THIRD EDITION

Vocabulary for GCSE GERMAN

Revised for the New GCSE specifications

Philip Horsfall and Ursula Horsfall

Nelson Thornes

Published in 2001 by:
Nelson Thornes Ltd
Delta Place
27 Bath Road
CHELTENHAM
GL53 7TH
United Kingdom

13 / 10 9 8

A catalogue record for this book is available from the British Library

ISBN 0 7487 6290 6

Page make-up by Tech Set Ltd

Printed in China

Acknowledgements

The authors and publisher would like to acknowledge the following for the use of
copyright material:

Süddeutsche Zeitung (p. 14); Südwest Presse Ulm (pp. 32 and 46); Deutsche
Telekom (p. 38); Verlag Deutsches Jugendherbergswerk (p. 62); Hotel Alpenrose
Oetz (p. 62); Frankfurter Allgemeine (p. 69); Stern (p. 79); Düsseldorfer Illustrierte
(p. 84).

Every effort has been made to trace copyright holders but the publisher will be
pleased to make the necessary arrangements at the first opportunity if there are any
omissions.

Contents

Introduction

You will need a wide vocabulary both to understand and to make yourself understood in a variety of situations in the GCSE German exam. You can use this book throughout Years 10 and 11, to help you find useful words and phrases for each German topic area, and to give you hints about how to learn vocabulary. This book sets out topic by topic the main vocabulary for **Foundation Tier** and **Higher Tier**. It can't include every word, as you may still meet some unknown words even at Foundation Tier, but you should be able to answer any question set without needing to know these unknown words. Each noun shows whether it is masculine (*der*), feminine (*die*) or neuter (*das*), and its plural is also shown in brackets. The words are grouped in short blocks of words that go together in some way, so that you will find them easier to learn.

Many of the words are presented in phrases which you could use in your speaking or writing exams, or when writing a letter. In the **School** section there is a list of German instructions you are likely to find at the start of questions in the exam. Word games and puzzles are provided to help you practise the words as well.

The Foundation words given in this book are taken from the four exam boards' lists for England and Wales. To make learning easier for you, some words and phrases are printed in red. These are important words and phrases that everybody should learn thoroughly because, in our opinion and experience, they are the most useful and the most likely to appear in your exam. However, these words and phrases form a minimum, so if you are aiming for a top grade, you will need to learn many of the other words as well.

The Higher words are also taken from the exam boards' lists. Some words are classified by one examination board as Foundation, but by another as Higher Tier. This book classifies these words as either Foundation or Higher, based on the authors' experience and judgement.

At the end of each topic area you will find a section called **How to learn**. This has two parts: **Vocabulary** and **How to use a dictionary**, for you to use when preparing for your exam or for coursework.

At the back of the book there are some blank pages where you can add any further words or phrases that you find useful.

The following websites, correct at time of printing, will also give you further help with learning vocabulary and other practice for your GCSE German examinations:

www.bbc.co.uk/education/gcsebitesize
www.learn.co.uk
www.juma.de
http://atschool.eduweb.co.uk/haberg/reallyusefulge/default.htm
www.vokabel.com
www.linguaweb.co.uk

This book incorporates the 1996 German spelling reforms.

Yourself and Others

PERSONAL DETAILS

◆ **Foundation words**

das Alter (-)	age	heißen	to be called
geboren	born	unterschreiben	to sign
der Geburtstag (e)	birthday	die Unterschrift (en)	signature
das Geburtsdatum (-daten)	birth date		
der Geburtsort (e)	birth place	der Familienstand	marital status
das Land ("er)	country	ledig	single
die Heimat (en)	home	verlobt	engaged
die Staatsangehörigkeit (en)	nationality	verheiratet	married
der Wohnort (e)	place of	heiraten	to marry
	residence	die Hochzeit (en)	wedding
		der Kuss ("e)	kiss
der Name (n)	name	lieben	to love
der Vorname (n)	first name	geschieden	divorced
der Familienname (n)	surname	evangelisch	Protestant
der Mädchenname (n)	maiden	katholisch	Catholic
	name	der Gott ("er)	God

◆ **Foundation phrases**

Ich heiße Ben mit Vornamen.	My first name's Ben.
Sie hat am vierten Mai Geburtstag.	Her birthday is on May 4.
Ich bin 1987 in Manchester geboren.	I was born in Manchester in 1987.
Meinen Geburtstag feiern wir zu Hause.	We celebrate my birthday at home.
Ich bin Engländer/Engländerin.	I'm English.
Sie ist seit einem Jahr verheiratet.	She's been married for a year.

Fill in your details on this form:

Vorname _____

Familienname _____

Geburtsdatum _____

Geburtsort _____

Staatsangehörigkeit _____

◆ **Higher words**

die Heimatstadt (-städte)	home town	die Ehe (n)	marriage
umziehen	to move house	der Namenstag (e)	Saint's day
stammen aus	to come from	der Nachname (n)	second name
der Steckbrief (e)	personal profile	wachsen	to grow
sich verloben	to get engaged	erwachsen	grown up

◆ **Higher phrases**

Mein Name schreibt sich mit zwei L. My name is spelled with two Ls.
Ich bin schon oft umgezogen. I've moved house a lot.

FAMILY AND FRIENDS

◆ **Foundation words**

kennen	to know	der Onkel (-)	uncle
die Familie (n)	family	der Sohn ("e)	son
die Eltern (pl)	parents	die Tochter (")	daughter
die Mutter (")	mother	der Schwiegersohn ("e)	son-in-law
die Mutti (s)	mum	die Schwiegertochter (")	daughter-in-law
der Vater (")	father		
der Vati (s)	dad	der Erwachsene (n)	adult
der Bruder (")	brother	die Erwachsene (n)	
die Schwester (n)	sister	die Frau (en)	woman, Mrs
die Geschwister (pl)	brothers and sisters	die Dame (n)	lady
		der Mann ("er)	man
		der Herr (en)	gentleman, Mr
die Großeltern (pl)	grandparents	der Rentner (-)	pensioner
die Großmutter (-mütter)	grandmother	die Rentnerin (nen)	
die Omi/Oma (s)	grandma		
der Großvater (-väter)	grandfather	das Einzelkind (er)	only child
der Opi/Opa (s)	grandad	das Baby (s)	baby
der Enkel (-)	grandson	das Kind (er)	child
die Enkelin (nen)	granddaughter	das Mädchen (-)	girl
		der Junge (n)	boy
der Verwandte (n)	relative	der Zwilling (e)	twin
die Verwandte (n)			
der Vetter (-)	cousin	das Mitglied (er)	member
die Kusine (n)		der Freund (e)	friend
der Neffe (n)	nephew	die Freundin (nen)	
die Nichte (n)	niece	der Partner (-)	partner
die Tante (n)	aunt	die Partnerin (nen)	

7

◆ Foundation phrases

Ich habe einen Bruder und eine Schwester.	I've got a brother and a sister.
Ich bin Einzelkind.	I'm an only child.
Meine Großeltern wohnen in Dorset.	My grandparents live in Dorset.
Ich habe viele Verwandte.	I've got lots of relatives.
Mein Vater ist wieder verheiratet.	My father has remarried.

◆ Higher words

die Ehefrau (en)	wife	der Halbbruder (¨)	half-brother
der Ehemann (¨er)	husband	die Halbschwester (n)	half-sister
das Ehepaar (e)	married couple	getrennt	separated
der Elternteil (e)	parent	der Witwer (-)	widower
der Familienangehörige (n)	family	die Witwe (n)	widow
die Familienangehörige (n)	member	die Senioren (pl)	senior citizens
der Stiefvater (¨)	stepfather	sterben	to die
die Stiefmutter (¨)	stepmother	tot	dead

◆ Higher phrases

Meine ältere Schwester ist ledig.	My elder sister is single.
Ich bin der/die Jüngste in der Familie.	I'm the youngest in the family.
Meine Eltern sind getrennt.	My parents are separated.

APPEARANCE

◆ Foundation words

aussehen	to look, appear	dünn	thin
das Auge (n)	eye	schlank	slim
das Haar (e)	hair	hässlich	ugly
der Bart (¨e)	beard	hübsch	pretty
der Schnurrbart (-bärte)	moustache	mittelgroß	medium-sized
die Brille (n)	glasses	schön	beautiful
die Glatze (n)	bald head	lang	long
die Zigarre (n)	cigar	kurz	short
die Zigarette (n)	cigarette	lockig	curly
die Pfeife (n)	pipe	glatt	straight
groß	tall		
dick	fat	*See page 44 for parts of the body.*	

◆ **Foundation phrases**

Er hat braune Augen und schwarzes Haar.	He's got brown eyes and black hair.
Er trägt eine Brille.	He wears glasses.
Mein Vater hat einen Bart.	My father has a beard.
Sie hat kurzes, lockiges Haar.	She's got short, curly hair.
Sie ist groß und schlank.	She's tall and slim.
Er sieht sehr dünn aus.	He looks very thin.

◆ **Higher words**

ähnlich	similar	erkennen	to recognise
gut aussehend	good-looking	der Pferdeschwanz ("e)	ponytail
das Gesicht (er)	face	das Piercing (s)	body piercing
der Teint (s)	complexion	der Lippenstift (e)	lipstick
der Pony (s)	fringe	vollschlank	plump

◆ **Higher phrases**

Sie ist mir sehr ähnlich.	She's very much like me.
Ich bin relativ klein.	I'm relatively short.
Ich habe sie kaum erkannt.	I hardly recognised her.

CHARACTER AND PERSONAL RELATIONSHIPS

◆ **Foundation words**

beliebt	popular	böse	angry
freundlich	friendly	zornig	angry
Humor haben	to have a sense of humour	frech	cheeky
		dumm	stupid
lustig	cheerful, funny	faul	lazy
sympathisch	friendly	arm	poor
froh	happy, merry	reich	rich
glücklich	happy	allein	alone
fleißig	hard-working		
intelligent	intelligent	geduldig	patient
brav	well-behaved	optimistisch	optimistic
nett	nice	pessimistisch	pessimistic
natürlich	natural	kritisieren	to criticise
schüchtern	shy	zufrieden	satisfied
		reif	mature
ärgerlich	annoying	unreif	immature

◆ **Foundation phrases**

Ich bin meistens freundlich, aber etwas schüchtern.	I'm usually friendly but a little shy.
Mein Bruder hat sehr viel Humor.	My brother's got a good sense of humour.
Er ist ein sympathischer Mensch.	He's a likeable person.

9

◆ Higher words

launisch	moody	gesellig	sociable
vernünftig	sensible	selbstsüchtig	selfish
gemein	mean	eingebildet	conceited
hilfsbereit	helpful	neidisch	envious
ungeduldig	impatient	angeberisch	boastful
bescheiden	modest		
ehrgeizig	ambitious	der Kummerkasten (kästen)	agony column
sich verstehen mit	to get on with	der Rat (Ratschläge)	advice
die Beziehung (en)	relationship	raten	to advise
die Freundschaft (en)	friendship	die Sorge (n)	problem
die Clique (n)	gang of friends	romantisch	romantic
die Eigenschaft (en)	quality, characteristic	verliebt sein	to be in love
		liebevoll	loving
die Laune (n)	mood	erröten	to blush
guter Laune sein	to be in a good mood	warmherzig	warm-hearted
		reizvoll	charming
schlechter Laune sein	to be in a bad mood	attraktiv	attractive
		rücksichtsvoll	considerate
das Gefühl (e)	feeling	verständnisvoll	understanding
sich ärgern	to get annoyed	nachdenklich	thoughtful
lügen	to lie	brav	well-behaved
die Lüge (n)	lie	zärtlich	gentle
der Streit (e)	argument	ehrlich	honest
nerven	to get on somebody's nerves	humorvoll	with a good sense of humour
		verantwortlich	responsible
höflich	polite	selbstbewusst	self-confident
sich schämen	to be ashamed	treu	faithful
vergesslich	absent-minded	untreu	unfaithful
gesprächig	chatty	das Vertrauen	trust
schwatzhaft	talkative	zuverlässig	reliable
kontaktfreudig	outgoing		

◆ Higher phrases

Ich lerne gern neue Leute kennen.	I like meeting new people.
Ich verstehe mich gut mit allen.	I get on well with everyone.
Ich vertrage mich gut mit meinen Eltern.	I get on well with my parents.
Manchmal ist er schlecht gelaunt.	Sometimes he's in a bad mood.
Ich kann sie nicht leiden.	I can't stand her.

Try filling in this form from a dating agency.

- ✄

Finden Sie Ihren idealen Partner!

Partner-Testbogen ♥

Bitte deutlich in Blockschrift ausfüllen

1. Herr ☐   Frau ☐

Nachname: _____

Vorname: _____

Str./Nr.: _____

PLZ/Ort: _____

2. Persönliche Auskünfte

Familienstand:

ledig ☐   gesch. ☐   verw. ☐   getr. lebend ☐

Staatsangehörigkeit: _____

Geburtsdatum: _____

Religion: _____

Geburtsort: _____

3. Ihre Eigenschaften

☐ häuslich   ☐ ehrgeizig   ☐ kinderlieb

☐ natürlich   ☐ humorvoll   ☐ strebsam

☐ romantisch   ☐ tierlieb   ☐ großzügig

☐ zärtlich   ☐ sparsam   ☐ freundlich

☐ schüchtern   ☐ ruhig   ☐ faul

Sonstiges: _____

Wie, glauben Sie, würden Menschen Sie beurteilen, die Sie gut kennen?

☐ ist zu jedem Spaß aufgelegt

☐ ist etwas verträumt

☐ hat nie Probleme

☐ nimmt das Leben schwer

☐ lässt sich durch nichts aus der Ruhe bringen

☐ ist immer aktiv

☐ redet gern und viel

4. Ihr Äußeres

Körpergröße in cm: _____

Haarfarbe: _____

Aussehen:

☐ solide   ☐ salopp   ☐ modisch

☐ elegant   ☐ repräsentativ   ☐ sportlich

5. Ihre Interessen

Geistig	Praktisch	Sportlich
☐ Musik	☐ Handarbeiten	☐ Bowling
☐ Theater	☐ Heimwerken	☐ Tennis
☐ Ballett	☐ Fotografieren	☐ Federball
☐ Oper	☐ Sammeln	☐ Squash
☐ Musical	☐ Kochen	☐ Gymnastik
☐ Kino	☐ Gartenarbeit	☐ Reiten
☐ Fernsehen	☐ Musizieren	☐ Fußball
☐ Literatur	☐ Tanzen	☐ Handball
Sonstiges:	Sonstiges:	Sonstiges:

_____

6. Wie soll Ihr zukünftiger Partner/ Ihre zukünftige Partnerin sein?

Mindestalter: _____

Größe: von _____ cm bis _____ cm egal ☐

Soll Ihr Wunsch-Partner zum großen Teil Ihre Interessen haben?   Ja ☐   Nein ☐   egal ☐

Unterschrift: _____

- ✄

PETS AND ANIMALS

◆ Foundation words

das Haustier (e)	pet	der Kanarienvogel (-vögel)	canary
der Hund (e)	dog	das Insekt (en)	insect
das Kaninchen (-)	rabbit	das Pferd (e)	horse
die Katze (n)	cat	die Kuh (¨e)	cow
die Maus (Mäuse)	mouse	das Schaf (e)	sheep
das Meerschweinchen (-)	guinea pig	das Schwein (e)	pig
der Wellensittich (e)	budgerigar		
der Fisch (e)	fish	beißen	to bite
die Schildkröte (n)	tortoise	füttern	to feed
die Schlange (n)	snake	fressen	to eat
der Vogel (¨)	bird	gehören	to belong to

◆ Foundation phrases

Ich habe keine Haustiere.	I haven't got any pets.
Ich habe einen Hund.	I've got a dog.
Ich mag Katzen nicht.	I don't like cats.
Ich hatte früher ein Kaninchen.	I used to have a rabbit.
Es ist vor zwei Jahren gestorben.	It died two years ago.

◆ Higher words

der Goldfisch (e)	goldfish	bellen	to bark
das Huhn (¨er)	hen, chicken	der Käfig (e)	cage
die Biene (n)	bee	der Stall (¨e)	stable
die Wespe (n)	wasp	neugierig	curious

◆ Higher phrases

Ich hätte gern einen Hund, aber mein Vater ist dagegen.	I'd like a dog, but my father's against it.

What do these signs mean?

BITTE DIE TIERE NICHT FÜTTERN

Vorsicht bissiger Hund!

H O W   T O   L E A R N

V O C A B U L A R Y
Write down the names of a friend, neighbour, some relatives, your pet, etc. Then write the correct word after them without looking them up. For example:

Denis ist mein Onkel.

Mrs Smith ist meine Nachbarin.

Agnes ist meine Großmutter.

H O W   T O   U S E   A   D I C T I O N A R Y
The plurals of nouns in German often cause problems. Your dictionary will tell you how to get the plural right, in the same way as this book does, by giving it in brackets after the noun. Where your dictionary has two sets of letters in brackets after the noun, it is the second set of letters that is the plural.

Practise with your dictionary so that you get the following plurals correct:

1 Ich habe zwei (brothers). ....

2 Ich habe viele (aunts). ....

3 Ich habe zwei (cats). ....

4 Ich habe blaue (eyes). ....

(Answer on page 98)

T I P P S   T I P P S   T I P P S

Home Life

◆ **Foundation words**

die Adresse (n)	address	das Dach (¨er)	roof
wohnen	to live	das Erdgeschoss	ground floor
die Wohnung (en)	flat	die Tür (en)	door
der Bungalow (s)	bungalow	klingeln	to ring
das Haus (Häuser)	house	klopfen	to knock
das Doppelhaus	semi-detached house	die Wand (¨e)	wall (indoors)
das Einfamilienhaus	detached house	die Mauer (n)	wall (outdoors)
das Hochhaus	high-rise block	der Garten (¨)	garden
das Reihenhaus	terraced house	die Hütte (n)	hut
der Wohnblock (-blöcke)	block of flats	das Holz (¨er)	wood
		der Rasen (-)	lawn
drinnen	indoors	die Blume (n)	flower
die Etage (n)	storey, floor	die Garage (n)	garage

◆ **Foundation phrases**

Wie ist deine Adresse?	What's your address?
Meine Adresse ist… Straße zwanzig.	My address is 20… Road.
Wir wohnen in einem Reihenhaus.	We live in a terraced house.
Ich wohne in einem Doppelhaus.	I live in a semi-detached house.
Mein Haus gefällt mir sehr, weil es modern ist.	I like my house a lot because it's modern.
Das Haus ist ziemlich klein.	The house is quite small.
Wir haben eine Garage und einen Garten.	We've got a garage and a garden.
Wir haben keinen Garten.	We haven't got a garden.
Es ist in der Stadtmitte.	It's in the town centre.
Ich wohne in einem Dorf auf dem Land.	I live in a village in the country.

What sorts of accommodation are being offered here?

Familienkomfort zum Wohlfühlen
Eigentumswohnungen
Ulm-Wiblingen
Lindauer Staße
Unser Angebot:
2-Zi.-Whgn. 61–67 m²
3-Zi.-Whgn. 87–93 m²
4-Zi.-Whgn. 93–113 m²

Gröbenzell
Einfamilienhaus ca. 150m² Wfl., ca. 60m²
Hobbyraum, 1,4 km zur S-Bahn,
beziehbar Frühjahr, € 648 000,– inkl Garage
Hülsebusch Imm. ☎ 089/8120886

Reihenhaus in Garching
E + 1 + ausgeb. Dachg. + Sout., Gge.,
Bj. 71, guter Zustand, 220m² Grd., 147m²

◆ **Higher words**

oben	upstairs	privat	private
unten	downstairs	luxuriös	luxury
die Terrasse (n)	patio	draußen	outside
das Tor (e)	gate	umziehen	to move house
mieten	to rent		
bauen	to build	ausstatten	to equip
die Eigentums-	owner-occupied	gemütlich	cosy
wohnung (en)	flat	heizen	to heat
der Mieter (-)	tenant	der Obstgarten (-gärten)	orchard
die Mieterin (nen)		malerisch	picturesque
die Sozialwohnung (en)	council housing	anbauen	to build an
das Zuhause (-)	home		extension
der Besitzer (-)	owner	der Rand (¨er)	edge
die Besitzerin (nen)		sich befinden	to be situated

◆ **Higher phrases**

Der Garten hat etwa 40 Quadratmeter.	The garden is about 40 square metres.
Wir wollen umziehen.	We want to move house.
Wir mieten das Gebäude.	We rent the building.
Wir wohnen im zweiten Stock.	We live on the second floor.
Unser Haus ist von Feldern umgeben.	Our house is surrounded by fields.
Die Küche ist gut ausgestattet.	The kitchen is well-equipped.
Wir wohnen am Stadtrand.	We live on the edge of town.
Es befindet sich neben einer Kirche.	It's situated next to a church.

AROUND THE HOME

◆ **Foundation words**

der Dachboden (-böden)	attic	das Klo (s)	loo
der Keller (-)	cellar	die Toilette (n)	toilet
die Diele (n)	hall	der Gang (¨e)	corridor
der Flur (e)	entrance hall	die Stufe (n)	step
das Badezimmer (-)	bathroom	die Treppe (n)	staircase
das Esszimmer (-)	dining room	der Boden (¨)	floor
die Küche (n)	kitchen	der Fußboden (-böden)	floor
der Waschraum (-räume)	utility room	die Decke (n)	ceiling
das Wohnzimmer (-)	living room	die Heizung (en)	heating
das Schlafzimmer (-)	bedroom	die Zentralheizung (en)	central heating
schlafen	to sleep		

◆ Foundation phrases

Es gibt ein Esszimmer und eine Küche.	There's a dining room and a kitchen.
Es hat drei Schlafzimmer.	It's got three bedrooms.
Die Toilette ist neben meinem Zimmer.	The toilet is next to my bedroom.
Das Wohnzimmer ist hier rechts.	The lounge is here on the right.

◆ Higher words

der Wintergarten (¨)	conservatory	das Leck (s)	leak
das Arbeitszimmer (-)	study	der Strom	electric current
der Treppenflur (e)	landing	die Steckdose (n)	socket
das Untergeschoss (e)	basement	der Stecker (-)	plug
teilen	to share	der Kamin (e)	fire-place
		die Leiter (n)	ladder
die Tapete (n)	wallpaper	der Fensterladen (¨)	shutter
tapezieren	to wallpaper	das Schloss (¨er)	lock
streichen	to paint	aufschließen	to unlock
der Hahn (¨e)	tap		

◆ Higher phrases

Ich habe mein eigenes Zimmer.	I've got my own room.
Ich muss das Zimmer mit meiner Schwester teilen.	I have to share the room with my sister.

FURNITURE

◆ Foundation words

die Möbel (pl)	furniture	das Bücherregal (e)	bookshelf
der Stuhl (¨e)	chair	der Schreibtisch (e)	desk
der Herd (e)	cooker	der Vorhang (-hänge)	curtain
der Schrank (¨e)	cupboard	der Wecker (-)	alarm clock
der Kühlschrank (¨e)	fridge		
die Waschmaschine (n)	washing machine	das Büffet (s)	sideboard
		der Tisch (e)	table
die Spülmaschine (n)	dishwasher	der Fernsehapparat (e)	television set
der Mikrowellenherd (e)	microwave oven	der Fernseher (-)	television set
der Ofen (¨)	oven	das Videogerät (e)	video player
		das Klavier (e)	piano
das Bett (en)	bed	die Lampe (n)	lamp
bequem	comfortable	der Lehnstuhl (¨e)	armchair
das Kopfkissen (-)	pillow	der Sessel (-)	armchair
der Kleiderschrank (¨e)	wardrobe	das Sofa (s)	sofa
der Spiegel (-)	mirror	der Teppich (e)	carpet
das Regal (e)	shelf	die Uhr (en)	clock

◆ **Higher words**

eingebaut	built-in	möbliert	furnished
das Kissen (-)	cushion	das Spülbecken (-)	sink
die Kommode (n)	chest of drawers	das Waschbecken (-)	washbasin
der Aschenbecher (-)	ash tray	die Gardine (n)	curtain
das Federbett (en)	duvet	das Elektrogerät (e)	electrical
die Bettdecke (n)	blanket		appliance
die Tischdecke (n)	table cloth		

◆ **Higher phrases**

Wir haben mein Zimmer neu möbliert. — We've refurnished my room.
Die Tapete passt gut zum Teppich. — The wallpaper matches the carpet.

DAILY ROUTINE

◆ **Foundation words**

das Bad ("er)	bath	aufstehen	to get up
das Badetuch (-tücher)	bath towel	sich waschen	to wash
die Badewanne (n)	bath tub	sich anziehen	to get dressed
nehmen	to take	sich ausziehen	to get undressed
die Dusche (n)	shower	sich umziehen	to get changed
duschen	to shower		
brauchen	to need	sich kämmen	to comb one's hair
das Handtuch (-tücher)	towel	sich die Haare bürsten	to brush one's hair
der Rasierapparat (e)	shaver	sich schminken	to put on make-up
die Seife (n)	soap		
der Spiegel (-)	mirror	essen	to eat
der Kamm ("e)	comb	trinken	to drink
das Waschbecken (-)	washbasin	das Frühstück (e)	breakfast
das Toilettenpapier	toilet paper	das Mittagessen (-)	lunch
die Wäsche	washing	das Abendessen (-)	evening meal
die Zahnpasta	toothpaste		
		die Kaffeepause (n)	coffee break
aufwachen	to wake up	verlassen	to leave

◆ **Foundation phrases**

Das Abendessen ist um sieben Uhr. — Dinner is at seven o'clock.
Wir frühstücken gegen acht Uhr. — We eat breakfast at about eight o'clock.
Brauchst du etwas? — Do you need anything?
Ich habe mein Handtuch vergessen. — I've forgotten my towel.
Ich habe keine Zahnpasta. — I haven't got any toothpaste.
Du findest die Seife im Badezimmer. — You'll find the soap in the bathroom.
Darf ich duschen? — May I have a shower?
Die Dusche ist neben dem Schlafzimmer. — The shower is next to the bedroom.

◆ Higher words

einschlafen	to fall asleep	der Nagellack (e)	nail varnish
sich rasieren	to have a shave	sich beeilen	to hurry up
sich ausruhen	to rest	der Fön (e)	hairdrier
sich abtrocknen	to dry oneself	bereit	ready

◆ Higher phrases

Gewöhnlich schlafe ich um elf Uhr ein.	I usually go to sleep at eleven o'clock.
Ich putze mir die Zähne.	I clean my teeth.
Ich trockne mich mit einem Handtuch ab.	I dry myself with a towel.

JOBS AROUND THE HOME

◆ Foundation words

die Hausarbeit	housework	abtrocknen	to dry up
helfen	to help	aufräumen	to tidy up
waschen	to wash	backen	to bake
spülen	to wash up	decken	to cover, set
abspülen	to wash up	kochen	to cook
abwaschen	to wash up	machen	to do, make
der Staubsauger (-)	vacuum cleaner	putzen	to clean
abräumen	to clear the table		

◆ Foundation phrases

Was machst du, um zu Hause zu helfen?	What do you do to help at home?
Ich spüle (ab).	I wash up.
Ich mache immer mein Bett.	I always make my bed.
Morgen werde ich mein Zimmer aufräumen.	Tomorrow I'll tidy up my room.
Meine Mutter macht fast alles.	My mother does almost everything.
Manchmal wasche ich das Auto.	I sometimes wash the car.

◆ Higher words

sauber machen	to clean	bügeln	to iron
kehren	to sweep	mähen	to mow
basteln	to do odd jobs	dreckig	dirty
das Bügeleisen (-)	iron	der Haushalt (e)	household

◆ Higher phrases

Ich helfe beim Einkaufen.	I help with the shopping.
Bügeln mache ich ungern.	I don't like ironing.
Mein Vater bereitet das Abendessen vor.	My father gets the evening meal ready.
Ab und zu mähe ich den Rasen.	I occasionally mow the lawn.

18

HOW TO LEARN

VOCABULARY

The umlaut is an essential part of German spelling. Vowels with umlauts (*ä, ö, ü*) are pronounced differently to those without (*a, o, u*). As you learn key phrases from each section, write them out without the umlauts, then see if you can fill them in correctly a day or so later.

See if you can put the umlauts correctly on these sentences:

1 Ich raume manchmal auf oder ich spule ab.

2 Wir fruhstucken in der Kuche.

3 Es gibt zwei Schranke uber meinem Bett.

(Answer on page 98)

HOW TO USE A DICTIONARY

One way of improving your dictionary use is to speed up your mastery of alphabetical work.

Write the words from this box in the correct alphabetical order as quickly as possible (if you can work with a partner, try this as a race):

> bürsten, Babysitter, bequem, brauchen,
>
> Büffet, Bücherregal, Bett, Badewanne,
>
> Badetuch, Blume, Boden, Bungalow

(Answer on page 98)

19

School

CLASSROOM OBJECTS

◆ Foundation words

der Bleistift (e)	pencil	das Lineal (e)	ruler
der Filzstift (e)	felt-tip pen	das Tonbandgerät (e)	tape recorder
der Füller (-)	pen		(reel to reel)
der Kugelschreiber (-)	ballpoint pen	der Kassettenrekorder	tape recorder
der Kuli (s)	biro	(-)	
der Stift (e)	pen	die Kassette (n)	tape
		die Kreide (-stücke)	chalk
das Buch (¨er)	book	der Schwamm (¨e)	sponge
das Wörterbuch (¨er)	dictionary	die Tafel (n)	board
das Heft (e)	exercise book	die Mappe (n)	schoolbag
der Ordner (-)	file	die (Schul)tasche (n)	(school)bag
das Papier (e)	paper	die Aktentasche (n)	briefcase
der Radiergummi (s)	rubber	der Taschenrechner (-)	calculator

◆ Foundation phrases

Ich habe keinen Kuli.	I haven't got a pen.
Ich habe mein Heft vergessen.	I've forgotten my exercise book.
Ich brauche ein neues Heft.	I need a new exercise book.

◆ Higher words

das Etui (s)	pencil case	das Blatt Papier (-)	sheet of paper
das Federmäppchen (-)	pencil case	die Büroklammer (n)	paper clip
der Klebstoff (e)	glue	der Locher (-)	hole punch
der Kleber (-)	glue stick		
die Tinte	ink	das Mikrofon (e)	microphone
die Patrone (n)	ink cartridge	der Kopfhörer (-)	headphones
der Tintenkiller (-)	eraser pen	der Tageslichtprojektor	OHP
der Korrekturstift (e)	correction pen	(en)	
das Klebeband (¨er)	sticky tape	der Feuerlöscher (-)	fire extinguisher

---

WORKING IN THE CLASSROOM

◆ Foundation words

der Fehler (-)	mistake	ausgezeichnet	excellent
die Verbesserung (en)	correction	dumm	stupid, silly
falsch	wrong		
richtig	right, correct	antworten	to answer
stimmen	to be right	die Antwort (en)	answer

fragen	to ask	die Liste (n)	list
die Frage (n)	question	kopieren	to copy
aufmachen	to open	sehen	to see
zumachen	to close	sprechen	to speak
arbeiten	to work	wiederholen	to repeat
aufnehmen	to record	lösen	to solve
aufpassen	to pay attention	vergessen	to forget
aufschreiben	to copy down	verstehen	to understand
zuhören	to listen	die Ahnung (en)	idea
buchstabieren	to spell	versuchen	to try
lesen	to read		
sagen	to say	die Hausaufgabe (n)	homework
schreiben	to write	vorbereiten	to prepare
zeichnen	to draw	sich umdrehen	to turn around
der Aufsatz (-sätze)	essay	die Schuluniform (en)	school uniform

◆ **Foundation phrases**

Wiederhole es bitte auf Deutsch.	Repeat that in German, please.
Sprechen Sie bitte langsamer.	Please speak more slowly.
Macht eure Bücher auf.	Open your books.
Arbeite mit einem Partner/einer Partnerin.	Work with a partner.
Seid ihr fertig?	Have you finished?
Wer fehlt?	Who's absent?
Ich habe meine Hausaufgaben nicht gemacht.	I haven't done my homework.
Ich habe jeden Abend eine Stunde Hausaufgaben zu machen.	I have one hour of homework every night.
Ich verstehe die Frage nicht.	I don't understand the question.
Ich habe keine Ahnung.	I've got no idea.
Wie schreibt man das?	How do you spell that?
Wie heißt das auf Englisch?	What's that in English?
Man muss die Schuluniform tragen.	You have to wear school uniform.
Ich finde die Schuluniform doof.	I think the school uniform is silly.

◆ **Higher words**

aussprechen	to pronounce	Recht haben	to be right
das Klassenbuch (-bücher)	register	Unrecht haben	to be wrong
		bedeuten	to mean
der Ausdruck (-drücke)	expression	ausrufen	to call out
diskutieren	to discuss	die Ruhe	quiet
korrigieren	to correct, mark	erklären	to explain

◆ Higher phrases

Ich komme mit meinem Klassenlehrer/ meiner Klassenlehrerin gut aus.	I get on well with my form tutor.
Die Stunde fällt aus.	The lesson is cancelled.
Samstags ist immer schulfrei.	We always have Saturdays off.
Wie spricht man das aus?	How do you pronounce that?
Was bedeutet dieser Ausdruck auf Englisch?	What does this expression mean in English?
Man darf in der Schule nicht rauchen.	You aren't allowed to smoke at school.
Es ist verboten, in den Gängen zu laufen.	Running in the corridors is forbidden.
Wir haben hitzefrei.	There's no school because it's too hot.

◆ Kreuzworträtsel

Gut, ein Haken! Meine Antwort muss (1) sein.

Ich arbeite in der Schule und zu Hause mache ich meine (2).

Ich weiß das Wort für »Essay« nicht mehr – ich habe es (3).

Ich verstehe nicht – ich habe keine (4).

Es stimmt nicht, also ist es (5).

Meine Bücher sind in meiner (6).

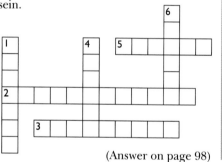

(Answer on page 98)

PLACES IN SCHOOL

◆ Foundation words

die Schule (n)	school	das Gymnasium (-sien)	grammar school
die Realschule (n)	secondary tech school	das Gebäude (-)	building
das Internat (e)	boarding school	der Schulhof (-höfe)	school yard
die Hauptschule (n)	elementary school	die Aula (Aulen)	hall
		die Bibliothek (en)	library
die Gesamtschule (n)	comprehensive school	die Kantine (n)	canteen
		das Klassenzimmer (-)	classroom
die Grundschule (n)	primary school	die Turnhalle (n)	sports hall, gym
		besuchen	to attend

◆ Foundation phrases

Ich besuche eine Gesamtschule.	I go to a comprehensive school.
Es gibt eine große Turnhalle.	There is a large sports hall.
Ich esse in der Kantine.	I eat in the school canteen.
Ich arbeite gern im Computerraum.	I like working in the computer room.

◆ Higher words

der Kindergarten (¨)	nursery school	das Sportzentrum	sports centre
das Labor (e)	laboratory	(-zentren)	
das Sprachlabor (e)	language lab	der Gang (¨e)	corridor
das Lehrerzimmer (-)	staffroom	der Umkleideraum	changing room
die Werkstatt (¨en)	workshop	(-räume)	
das Sekretariat (e)	school office	die Bühne (n)	stage
das Schulgelände (-)	school grounds	das schwarze Brett	noticeboard
		das Schließfach (¨er)	locker

SUBJECTS

◆ Foundation words

das Fach (¨er)	subject	malen	to paint
das Wahlfach (-fächer)	option	die Musik	music
die Stunde (n)	lesson	die Erdkunde	geography
der Stundenplan (-pläne)	timetable	die Geografie	geography
der Unterricht	lesson	die Geschichte	history
beginnen	to begin	die Religion	R.E.
dauern	to last	die Sprache (n)	language
enden	to end	die Fremdsprache (n)	foreign language
die Naturwissenschaft (en)	science	Französisch	French
die Biologie	biology	Latein	Latin
die Chemie	chemistry	Spanisch	Spanish
die Physik	physics	Englisch	English
die Mathe(matik)	maths	Deutsch	German
rechnen	to calculate	der Sport	sport
zählen	to count	das Turnen	P.E.
die Zahl (en)	number	die Sozialkunde	social science
die Informatik	I.T.	die Technik	technology
das Drama	drama	das Werken	technology
die Kunst	art	die Wirtschaftslehre	economics

◆ Foundation phrases

Die Schule beginnt um Viertel vor neun.	School begins at a quarter to nine.
Die erste Stunde beginnt um halb neun.	The first lesson starts at half past eight.
Die Schule ist um halb vier aus.	School ends at half past three.
Wir haben sechs Stunden am Tag.	We have six lessons a day.
Jede Stunde dauert fünfzig Minuten.	Each lesson lasts fifty minutes.
Montags haben wir Erdkunde.	We have geography on Mondays.
Mein Lieblingsfach ist Informatik.	My favourite subject is I.T.
Ich mache Geschichte nicht sehr gern.	I don't like doing history.
Ich mache Deutsch als Wahlfach.	I'm doing German as an option.

What subjects are on these stickers?

◆ **Higher words**

das Pflichtfach (¨er)	compulsory subject	aufgeben	to give up
die Ziffern (pl)	figures	obligatorisch	compulsory
abwählen	to drop	nachholen	to catch up

◆ **Higher phrases**

Deutsch haben wir als Pflichtfach.	German is a compulsory subject.
Ich lerne seit zwei Jahren Französisch.	I've been learning French for two years.
Ich werde Geschichte aufgeben.	I'll give up history.
Ich mache insgesamt acht Fächer.	I'm studying eight subjects altogether.
Ich spreche fließend Französisch.	I speak fluent French.

EXAMS AND TESTS

◆ **Foundation words**

prüfen	to test	üben	to practise
die Prüfung (en)	exam	die Übung (en)	practice, activity, exercise
die Abschlussprüfung (en)	final exam		
das Examen (-)	exam	erfolgreich	successful
die Arbeit	work, test	die Note (n)	mark
die Klassenarbeit (en)	test	die Qualifikation (en)	qualification
der Test (s)	test	das Zeugnis (se)	report
die Regel (n)	rule	durchfallen	to fail
das Abitur	A-levels	mangelhaft	poor, fail grade
lernen	to learn	befriedigend	satisfactory
übersetzen	to translate		

◆ **Foundation phrases**

Ich habe Klassenarbeiten nicht gern.	I don't like tests.
Ich brauche eine gute Note in Englisch.	I need a good grade in English.
In Physik werde ich sicher durchfallen.	I'll certainly fail physics.

◆ **Higher words**

die Oberstufe	Years 11, 12 and 13	der Realschulabschluss (-schlüsse)	GCSE equivalent
der Kurs (e)	course	die Hochschulreife	A-levels
bestehen	to pass	das Gespräch (e)	conversation
schriftlich	written	gestresst	stressed
mündlich	oral	enttäuscht	disappointed
die Nachhilfe	extra tuition	die Leistung (en)	achievement
sitzen bleiben	to repeat a year	der Leistungsdruck	pressure to do well
die Probeprüfung (en)	mock examination	der Erfolg (e)	success
das Ergebnis (se)	result	schaffen	to work
die Stufe (en)	level, stage	pauken	to revise
die Mittlere Reife (sing.)	GCSE equivalent	gratulieren	to congratulate
		abschreiben	to copy
		mogeln	to cheat
		schummeln	to cheat

◆ **Higher phrases**

Ich mache vielleicht einen GNVQ-Kurs.	Perhaps I'll do a GNVQ course.
Ich hoffe, die Prüfung zu bestehen.	I hope to pass the exam.
Ich habe viel geschafft.	I've done a lot of work.
Im Moment bin ich sehr gestresst!	I'm stressed out at the moment!
Ich muss mir zu viel merken.	I have to remember too much.

EXAM LANGUAGE

Ändere... den Text	**Change...** the text
Beantworte... die Fragen	**Answer...** the questions
Beschreibe... die Bilder	**Describe...** the pictures
... was du gemacht hast	... what you did
Ergänze... die Tabelle	**Complete...** the table
Erkläre... was passiert ist	**Explain...** what has happened
... was du gemacht hast	... what you did
Ersetze... die Bilder durch Wörter	**Replace...** the pictures with words
Erzähle... was passiert ist	**Say...** what has happened
Fülle... die Tabelle **aus**	**Fill in...** the table
... die Lücken **aus**	... the gaps
... das Formular **aus**	... the form
... die Sprechblasen **aus**	... the speech bubbles
Gib... Informationen über	**Give...** information about
Hake... die richtige Antwort **ab**	**Tick...** the correct answer
... den richtigen Buchstaben **ab**	... the correct letter

Hör... das Gespräch **an**	**Listen to...** the conversation
... das Interview **an**	... the interview
Kreuze... die richtige Antwort **an**	**Tick...** the right answer
Korrigiere... die folgenden Sätze	**Correct...** the following sentences
Lies... den Artikel **durch**	**Read...** the article
Mache... eine Liste	**Make...** a list
... einen Kreis	... a circle
... einen Haken/ein Kreuz	... a tick/cross
Markiere... die richtige Antwort	**Mark...** the correct answer
Ordne... die Bilder	**Put...** the pictures in order
Schreibe... eine Antwort auf den Brief	**Write...** an answer to the letter
... einen Bericht	... a report
... die richtige Nummer auf den Plan	... the right number on the map
Sieh... die Bilder **an**	**Look at...** the pictures
Stell Fragen über...	**Ask** questions about...
Stell dir vor, dass...	**Imagine** that...
Suche... die richtigen Nummern	**Look for...** the right numbers
Trage... den Namen in das Kästchen **ein**	**Place...** the name in the box
Unterstreiche...	**Underline...**
Verbinde... die Satzteile	**Join up...** the parts of the sentence
Vergleiche... diese Sätze mit dem Text	**Compare...** these sentences with the text
Wähle... den passenden Satz	**Choose...** the correct sentence
Was passt zusammen?	**What** goes together/matches?
Welches Wort fehlt?	**Which** word is missing?

OUT OF LESSONS

◆ Foundation words

die Pause (n)	break	die Klassenfahrt (en)	class trip
die Mittagspause (n)	lunch break	das Trimester (-)	term
der Austausch (e)	exchange visit	bestrafen	to punish

◆ Foundation phrases

Die Mittagspause beginnt um halb eins.	Lunch time begins at half past twelve.
In der Mittagspause spreche ich mit Freunden.	At lunch time I talk to friends.

◆ Higher words

die Unterhaltung (en)	conversation	die Schulreise (n)	school trip
die Versammlung (en)	assembly	schulfrei	no school
das Schulsportfest (e)	sports day	schwänzen	to play truant
das Schulfest (e)	school fête	nachsitzen	to get detention
der Elternabend (e)	parents' evening	sich unterhalten	to chat
		plaudern	to chat

◆ Higher phrases

Nächste Woche haben wir schulfrei.	There's no school next week.
Wir machen eine Klassenfahrt nach London.	We're going on a class trip to London.

What's happening at this school fête?

SCHULFEST

Tombola, Theater, Modenschau, Musik, Sport, Disco, Grillstation, Kaffeestube, Eisdiele und vieles mehr!

Freitag, 27. Mai, 14.00 Uhr
Montabaur,
Von-Bodelschwingh-Straße
(Schulzentrum)

Ab 18.00 Uhr Konzert der bekannten Gruppe: BÜRGSCHAFT.

Es laden ein:
Schüler und Lehrer
der Berufsbildenden Schule Montabaur.

Eintritt frei!

DESCRIBING SCHOOL AND PEOPLE

◆ Foundation words

der Assistent (en) die Assistentin (nen)	assistant	die Aufsicht	supervision
der Schuldirektor (en) die Schuldirektorin (nen)	head teacher	kompliziert	complicated
		einfach	easy
der Hausmeister (-)	caretaker	schwer	difficult
die Klasse (n)	class	schwierig	difficult
der Klassensprecher (-) die Klassensprecherin (nen)	form rep	interessant	interesting
		sich langweilen	to get bored
		langweilig	boring
der Lehrer (-) die Lehrerin (nen)	teacher	pünktlich	punctual
		fleißig	hard-working
der Schüler (-) die Schülerin (nen)	pupil	klug	clever
		streng	strict
der Schultag (e)	school day		

◆ Foundation phrases

Ich mag Mathe, weil der Lehrer toll ist.	I like maths because the teacher is great.
Englisch gefällt mir, weil es einfach ist.	I like English because it's easy.
Die Schule gefällt mir sehr.	I like school a lot.
Ich mag meine Schule nicht. Sie ist zu groß.	I don't like my school. It's too big.
Ich bin nicht sehr gut in Mathe.	I'm not very good at maths.
Ich finde Musik langweilig.	I think music is boring.

◆ Higher words

der Putzmann (-männer)	cleaner	die Schülervertretung (en)	student representation
die Putzfrau (en)		der Streber (-)	swot
der Schulleiter (-)	head teacher	die Streberin (nen)	
die Schulleiterin (nen)			
die Ganztagsschule (n)	school in the morning and afternoon	unterrichten	to teach
		bestrafen	to punish
		anstrengend	tiring
der Unterricht	lessons, teaching	diszipliniert	disciplined
		faul	lazy
der Stress	stress	frech	cheeky
die Strafarbeit (en)	extra written work (punishment)	gemischt	mixed
		nützlich	useful
		streng	strict
		sympathisch	likeable

◆ Higher phrases

Unsere Mathelehrerin ist sympathisch.	Our maths teacher is nice.
Die Naturwissenschaften finde ich anstrengend.	I find science hard work.
Ich besuche eine gemischte Gesamtschule.	I go to a mixed comprehensive.
Seit langem haben wir einen Aushilfslehrer für Mathe.	We've had a supply teacher for maths for a long time.

HOW TO LEARN

VOCABULARY

When you learn new words, set yourself some small tests to see how well you have learned them. One way is to make up anagrams by jumbling up the letters in a word or phrase. You then try to solve your own anagrams the next day. To start you off, have a go at these anagrams:

homework = SUUAANEGHFAB (Hausaufgaben in the wrong order)

1 *canteen* = DIE NIKATEN ....

2 *lessons* = DIE NNTSUED ....

3 *English is my favourite subject* = SCLINEGH SIT INME FLICEHBLIGNSA

....

4 *It's not hard* = SE TIS ITHCN REHSCW ....

....

(Answer on page 98)

HOW TO USE A DICTIONARY

At the end of any written work, your dictionary could help you to check the spelling of words. Look at this short section of a letter, and use a dictionary to find and correct the three words spelled wrongly:

> Ich finde Musik langwielig, aber
> ich lerne Gesichte sehr gern.
> Samestags ist immer schulfrei.

(Answer on page 98)

29

The World of Work

◆ Foundation words

die Zukunft	future	die Oberstufe (n)	sixth form
das Abitur	A-levels	der Student (en)	student (higher
die Ausbildung	education	die Studentin (nen)	education)
das Diplom (e)	degree	studieren	to study (higher
der Beruf (e)	profession		education)
der Job (s)	job	weiterlernen	to carry on
arbeiten	to work		studying (at
der Lehrling (e)	apprentice		school)
das Arbeitspraktikum	work	die Universität (en)	university
(-ka)	experience	die Uni (s)	uni

◆ Foundation phrases

Ich weiß nicht, was ich machen werde.	I don't know what I'll do.
Ich möchte weiterlernen.	I'd like to continue to study.
Ich bleibe auf der Schule.	I'm going to stay at school.
Ich möchte die Schule verlassen.	I'd like to leave school.
Ich will eine Stelle als Lehrling finden.	I want to find a place as an apprentice.
Ich habe keine Pläne.	I haven't got any plans.
Ich gehe nächstes Jahr auf eine weiterführende Schule.	I'm going to college next year.
Ich habe in einem Geschäft gearbeitet.	I worked in a shop.

◆ Higher words

die Erfahrung (en)	experience	die Lehre (n)	apprenticeship
die Erziehung	education	der Kurs (e)	course
der Lehrgang (¨e)	course	die Fachschule (n)	technical
die Zukunftspläne (pl)	plans for the		college
	future	die Hochschule (n)	college,
die Berufsausbildung	vocational		university
	training	der Studienplatz	university
die Berufsschule (n)	technical	(-plätze)	place
	college		

◆ Higher phrases

Ich will mit Leuten arbeiten.	I want to work with people.
Ich möchte im Ausland arbeiten.	I'd like to work abroad.
Ich habe schon eine Stelle gefunden.	I've already found a job.
Studieren interessiert mich nicht.	I'm not interested in studying.
Ich habe noch keine festen Pläne.	I don't have any definite plans yet.
Ich hoffe, dass ich später auf die Uni gehen kann.	I hope I can go to university later.

CAREERS AND EMPLOYMENT

◆ Foundation words

der Angestellte (n)	employee	der Briefträger (-)	postperson
die Angestellte (n)		die Briefträgerin (nen)	
der Beamte (n)	official, clerk	der Chef (s)	boss
die Beamtin (nen)		die Chefin (nen)	
der Arbeiter (-)	worker	der Elektriker (-)	electrician
die Arbeiterin (nen)		die Elektrikerin (nen)	
der Arbeitnehmer (-)	employee	der Fotograf (en)	photographer
die Arbeitnehmerin (nen)		die Fotografin (nen)	
der Kollege (n)	colleague	der Friseur (e)	hairdresser
die Kollegin (nen)		die Friseuse (n)	
		der Ingenieur (e)	engineer
der Hausmann (-männer)	house-husband	die Ingenieurin (nen)	
		die Polizei	police force
die Hausfrau (en)	housewife	der Polizist (en)	police officer
der Kaufmann (-männer)	businessman	die Polizistin (nen)	
die Kauffrau (en)	business-woman	der Bauer (n)	farmer
		die Bäuerin (nen)	
die Kaufleute (pl)	businesspeople	der Landarbeiter (-)	farm worker
der Kellner (-)	waiter	die Landarbeiterin (nen)	
die Kellnerin (nen)	waitress		
der Krankenpfleger (-)	nurse	die Abteilung (en)	department
die Krankenschwester (n)		das Büro (s)	office
der Sekretär (e)	secretary	die Fabrik (en)	factory
die Sekretärin (nen)		der Betrieb (e)	company
der Mechaniker (-)	mechanic	die Firma (Firmen)	company
die Mechanikerin (nen)		der Handel	trade
der Verkäufer (-)	sales assistant	halbtags	half-day
die Verkäuferin (nen)		der Arbeitgeber (-)	employer
		die Arbeitgeberin (nen)	

◆ Foundation phrases

Meine Mutter ist Sekretärin.	My mother is a secretary.
Mein Vater ist Friseur.	My father is a hairdresser.
Meine Schwester ist Hausfrau.	My sister is a housewife.
Sie arbeitet in einem Büro.	She works in an office.
Er arbeitet in einer Fabrik.	He works in a factory.
Sie arbeitet bei Tesco.	She works for Tesco.

What jobs are being advertised here?

STELLENANZEIGEN

*kika geht nach Oberösterreich und
eröffnet Mitte des Jahres in Linz das
14. Möbelhaus. Das schönste.*

**Ein neuer Job
im neuen Jahr:**

VERKÄUFER(INNEN)

EINRICHTUNGSBERATER(INNEN)

KASSIERER(INNEN)

TISCHLER(INNEN)

LAGERLEITER(INNEN)

EXPEDIENTEN

Wir stellen ein:

KRAFTFAHRER

mit Führerschein Kl. II.
Telefonische
Kontaktaufnahme unter
(0731) 492-245

Büro-Kauffrau

mit guten SM-Kenntnissen für sofort
nach Ulm gesucht.
Ausführliche Bewerbung unter PU 07910

◆ Higher words

die Karriere (n)	career
der Bäcker (-)	baker
die Bäckerin (nen)	
der Tischler (-)	carpenter
die Tischlerin (nen)	
der Anstreicher (-)	painter
die Anstreicherin (nen)	
der Gärtner (-)	gardener
die Gärtnerin (nen)	
der Blumenhändler (-)	florist
die Blumenhändlerin (nen)	
der Altenpfleger (-)	old people's
die Altenpflegerin (nen)	nurse
der Fabrikarbeiter (-)	factory worker
die Fabrikarbeiterin (nen)	
der Modezeichner (-)	fashion
die Modezeichnerin (nen)	illustrator
der Dolmetscher (-)	interpreter
die Dolmetscherin (nen)	
der Soldat (en)	soldier
die Soldatin (nen)	
der Chirurg (en)	surgeon
die Chirurgin (nen)	
der Rechtsanwalt (-wälte)	lawyer
die Rechtsanwältin (nen)	

der Richter (-)	judge
die Richterin (nen)	
der Landwirt (e)	farmer
die Landwirtin (nen)	
der Gewerkschaftler (-)	trade unionist
die Gewerkschaftlerin (nen)	
der Streikende (n)	striker
die Streikende (n)	
selbstständig	self-employed
gut bezahlt	well-paid
die Schichtarbeit	shiftwork
die Arbeitslosigkeit	unemployment
erfahren	experienced
beschäftigt	busy
erhalten	to receive
das Gehalt (¨er)	salary
der Lohn (¨e)	pay, wages
der Arbeitsplatz (-plätze)	place of work
jobben	to have a (casual) job
die Beförderungs- möglichkeit (en)	chance of promotion

32

◆ **Higher phrases**

Sie ist beruflich unterwegs.	She's away on business.
berufstätig sein	to be working
Ich möchte viele Erfahrungen sammeln.	I'd like to broaden my experience.
Er ist nicht im Dienst.	He's not on duty.

LOOKING FOR A JOB

◆ **Foundation words**

das Formular (e)	form	die Stellenanzeige (n)	job advert
ausfüllen	to fill in	der Termin (e)	appointment
sich bewerben (um)	to apply (for)	die Stelle (n)	job
die Chance (n)	chance	arbeitslos	unemployed
der Lebenslauf (-läufe)	CV	aufgeben	to give up

◆ **Foundation phrases**

Ich möchte Krankenschwester werden.	I'd like to become a nurse.
Er möchte eine Stelle als Mechaniker.	He'd like to work as a mechanic.
Mein Bruder ist arbeitslos.	My brother is unemployed.
Er kann keine Stelle finden.	He can't find a job.

◆ **Higher words**

die Qualifikation (en)	qualification	das Bewerbungs-	application
qualifiziert	qualified	formular (e)	form
die Aussichten (pl)	prospects	die Bewerbung (en)	application
die Berufsberatung	careers advice	das Vorstellungs-	job interview
das Antragsformular (e)	application form	gespräch (e)	

◆ **Higher phrases**

Ich möchte keine langen Arbeitszeiten.	I don't want to work long hours.
Ich suche einen Beruf mit Verantwortung.	I'm looking for a job with responsibility.
Ich halte viel Freizeit für wichtig.	I think a lot of free time is important.
Ich habe schon in einem Supermarkt gearbeitet.	I've already done some work in a supermarket.

33

C O M P U T E R S

◆ **Foundation words**

der Computer (-)	computer	die Software	software
der Bildschirm (e)	screen	programmieren	to program
der Drucker (-)	printer	speichern	to save
die Tastatur (en)	keyboard	der Tippfehler (-)	typing mistake
die Taste (n)	computer key		
die Diskette (n)	floppy disk	die E-Mail (s)	e-mail
die CD-ROM (s)	CD-ROM	die Webseite (n)	web page
		surfen	to surf

◆ **Foundation phrases**

Ich surfe sehr gern.   I love surfing the net.
Ich schreibe per E-Mail.   I write by e-mail.

◆ **Higher words**

das Passwort (-wörter)	password	die Computeranlage (en)	computer system
die Datei (en)	file		
die Datenbank (en)	data-base	die Textverarbeitung	word-processing
die Festplatte (n)	hard drive		
das CD-ROM-Laufwerk (e)	CD-ROM drive	formatieren	to format
		bearbeiten	to edit, adapt
das Diskettenlaufwerk (e)	floppy disk drive	kopieren	to copy
der Mikrochip (s)	microchip	löschen	to delete
das Internet	internet	herunterladen	to download
das Internetshopping	online shopping	hacken	to hack

◆ **Higher phrases**

Ich kann Musik herunterladen.   I can download music.
Ich schreibe alle meine Aufsätze mit   I word-process all my essays.
Textverarbeitung.

P O C K E T   M O N E Y

◆ **Foundation words**

das Taschengeld	pocket money	verdienen	to earn
sparen	to save	der Samstagsjob (s)	Saturday job
bekommen	to get	austragen	to deliver

◆ **Foundation phrases**

Ich habe einen Job.	I've got a job.
Ich trage Zeitungen aus.	I deliver newspapers.
Samstags arbeite ich als Kellner/in.	I work as a waiter/waitress on Saturdays.
Ich arbeite auch in einem Supermarkt.	I also work in a supermarket.
Ich arbeite vier Stunden.	I work for four hours.
Ich arbeite als Babysitter/in.	I work as a babysitter.
Ich bekomme drei Pfund pro Stunde.	I get three pounds an hour.
Ich finde es sehr interessant.	I find it very interesting.
Es ist langweilig, aber ich brauche das Geld.	It's boring but I need the money.
Die Arbeit gefällt mir sehr.	I like the job a lot.
Ich spare mein Geld.	I save my money.

◆ **Higher words**

der Ferienjob (s)	holiday job	zufrieden	satisfied
der Teilzeitjob (s)	part-time job	im Freien	in the open air
das Trinkgeld (er)	tip	schlecht bezahlt	badly paid

◆ **Higher phrases**

Ich zahle das Geld auf mein Konto ein.	I pay the money into my account.
Ich finde die Arbeit sehr uninteressant.	I find the work very uninteresting.
Ich arbeite seit zwei Monaten da.	I've been working there for two months.

Read these survey results about pocket money.

Eine Umfrage bei mehr als 700 Schülern/ Schülerinnen erbrachte diese Resultate:

1 Schüler(innen), die wöchentlich bis zu fünf Stunden arbeiten, besuchen die Schule regelmäßiger als die, die mehr als zehn Stunden arbeiten.

2 Schüler(innen), die bis zu fünf Stunden arbeiten, bleiben eher auf der Schule und machen Abitur.

3 Schüler(innen), die bis zu fünf Stunden arbeiten, haben bessere Noten in ihren GCSE-Prüfungen als die Schüler(innen), die mehr als zehn Stunden arbeiten.

HOW TO LEARN

VOCABULARY

To make learning German vocabulary more manageable, you need to decide which words are most important for you. Clearly if your father is an employee in a bank, then *der Bankangestellte* is a word you ought to know. The word *der Fleischer* may be less necessary. You need to spend more time learning words like *Büro* and *arbeitslos*, which are more likely to appear in the texts you meet, than *Betrieb* or *Lebenslauf*.

Put these eight words to do with further education and work into the two categories. Compare your answers with those suggested on page 98.

Very useful for GCSE   **Less useful for GCSE**

....

....

....

....

die Stelle
die Schichtarbeit
der Dolmetscher
die Firma
verdienen
die Bewerbung
die Abteilung
das Taschengeld

HOW TO USE A DICTIONARY

Many jobs in German have a masculine and a feminine form. The most common way of showing this is the *-in* ending on words showing the feminine.
For example: *der Lehrer* = male teacher and *die Lehrerin* = female teacher.

There are a few exceptions, for example:
• *die Friseuse*
• short words like *Arzt* and *Koch* add an umlaut: *die Ärztin*, *die Köchin*
• words that end in *-mann* change to *-frau*: *der Geschäftsmann* (businessman) becomes *die Geschäftsfrau* (businesswoman).

Complete these sentences describing what some women do for a living:

1 Er ist Sekretär und sie ist   ....

2 Er ist Polizist und sie ist   ....

3 Er ist Kellner und sie ist   ....

(Answer on page 98)

Services and the Media

POST

◆ Foundation words

die Ansichtskarte (n)	postcard	der Absender (-)	sender
die Postkarte (n)	postcard	die Anschrift (en)	address
der Brief (e)	letter	die Postleitzahl (en)	postal code
der Briefkasten (¨)	letter box	schicken	to send
die Briefmarke (n)	stamp	abschicken	to send off
kosten	to cost	einwerfen	to post
die Post	post office	die Luftpost	air mail
der Schalter (-)	counter		

◆ Foundation phrases

Gibt es eine Post hier in der Nähe?	Is there a post office near here?
Wo ist der Briefkasten?	Where is the letter box?
Ich möchte einen Brief nach England schicken.	I'd like to send a letter to England.
Was kostet ein Brief nach England?	How much is a letter to England?
Eine Briefmarke zu 60 Cent, bitte.	One 60-cent stamp, please.
Wann wird der Brief ankommen?	When will the letter arrive?

◆ Higher words

nachsenden	to send on, forward	der Briefträger (-) die Briefträgerin (nen)	postperson
das Paket (e)	parcel	der Briefwechsel (-)	correspondence
das Päckchen (-)	small parcel	erhältlich	available
beilegen	to enclose	die Postanweisung (en)	postal order
		die Telefonkarte (n)	phonecard

◆ Higher phrases

Wann ist die letzte Leerung?	When's the last collection?
Gehen Sie bitte zum Schalter 7.	Please go to counter 7.
einen Brief per Einschreiben schicken	to send a letter recorded delivery

T E L E P H O N E

◆ **Foundation words**

der Fernsprecher (-)	public phone	die Vorwahl(nummer)	dialling code
der Apparat (e)	phone	auflegen	to hang up
das Telefon (e)	phone	außer Betrieb	out of order
die Telefonzelle (n)	phone box	besetzt	engaged
der Anruf (e)	phone call	der Hörer (-)	receiver
anrufen	to call, ring	versuchen	to try
telefonieren	to phone	auf Wiederhören	bye (on phone)
der Anrufbeantworter (-)	answerphone	ausrichten	to give a message
wählen	to dial		
die Telefonnummer (n)	phone number		

◆ **Foundation phrases**

Gibt es ein Telefon in der Nähe?	Is there a phone nearby?
Könnte ich bitte meine Eltern anrufen?	May I phone my parents, please?
Wie ist Ihre Telefonnummer?	What's your phone number?
Kennen Sie die Vorwahlnummer?	Do you know the area code?
Helga am Apparat.	Helga speaking.
Kann ich bitte mit Herrn Rößner sprechen?	May I speak to Mr Rößner, please?
Ist Renate da?	Is Renate there?
Kann ich ihm etwas ausrichten?	Can I take a message for him?
Kann er mich zurückrufen?	Can he call me back?

What countries are listed on this leaflet?

☎ Die Vorwahlnummern für Ihre Auslandsgespräche nach:

Belgien	00 32	Niederlande	00 31
CSFR	00 42	Norwegen	00 47
Dänemark	00 45	Österreich	00 43
Finnland	00 358	Polen	00 48
Frankreich	00 33	Portugal	00 351
Griechenland	00 30	Schweden	00 46
Großbritannien	00 44	Schweiz	00 41
Irland	00 353	Spanien	00 34
Italien	00 39	Türkei	00 90
Luxemburg	00 352	USA	00 1

◆ **Higher words**

das Telefonbuch (-bücher)	directory	das Handy (s)	mobile phone
das Ferngespräch (e)	long-distance call	die Telefonkarte (n)	phone card
die Verbindung (en)	connection	der Notruf (e)	emergency call
verbinden	to connect	der Notdienst (e)	emergency service
faxen	to fax		

◆ **Higher phrases**

Kann ich Sie telefonisch erreichen?	Can I get you on the phone?
Ich versuche, Sie zu verbinden.	I'm trying to connect you.
Sie sind falsch verbunden.	You've got the wrong number.
Bitte warten!	Please hold the line!

BANK

◆ **Foundation words**

der Scheck (s)	cheque	das Kleingeld	change
der Reisescheck (s)	traveller's cheque	wechseln	to change
die Scheckkarte (n)	banker's card	die Wechselstube (n)	*bureau de change*
der Schein (e)	(bank)note	der Geldwechsel	exchange (money)
die Banknote (n)	(bank)note	das Konto (Konten)	account

◆ **Higher words**

der Wechselkurs (e)	exchange rate	abheben	to withdraw
der Euroscheck (s)	Eurocheque	sich erkundigen	to enquire
die Währung (en)	currency	umtauschen	to change
das Bargeld	cash	gebührenfrei	free of charge
die Gebühr (en)	fee	gebührenpflichtig	chargeable

◆ **Higher phrases**

Ich möchte diesen Scheck einlösen.	I'd like to cash this cheque.
Auf wen soll ich den Scheck ausstellen?	Who should I make the cheque out to?
Wie viel darf ich abheben?	How much can I take out?
Ich zahle regelmäßig Geld auf mein Konto ein.	I regularly pay money into my account.
Ich gebe viel/wenig Geld aus.	I spend a lot of/not much money.
Wie ist der Wechselkurs heute?	What's the exchange rate today?

LOST PROPERTY OFFICE

◆ Foundation words

das Fundbüro (s)	lost property office	der Fotoapparat (e)	camera
verlieren	to lose	der Regenschirm (e)	umbrella
vergessen	to leave (behind)	der Pass ("e)	passport
		die Halskette (n)	necklace
das Portemonnaie (s)	purse	die Uhr (en)	watch
die Tasche (n)	bag	der Ring (e)	ring
die Handtasche (n)	handbag	der Ohrring (e)	earring
die Brille (n)	pair of glasses	das Armband (-bänder)	bracelet
die Sonnenbrille (n)	pair of sunglasses	die Marke (n)	make
		ausfüllen	to fill in
der Koffer (-)	suitcase	das Formular (e)	form

◆ Foundation phrases

Ich habe ihn/sie/es/sie vergessen.	I left it/them behind.
Ich habe eine Tasche verloren.	I've lost a bag.
Ich habe sie im Bus gelassen.	I left it on the bus.
Mein Portemonnaie ist rot.	My purse is red.
Haben Sie einen grünen Regenschirm, bitte?	Have you got a green umbrella please?

◆ Higher words

bemerken (, dass)	to realise (that)	zurückgeben	to give back
abgeben	to hand in		

◆ Higher phrases

Ich habe einen schwarzen Lederkoffer verloren.	I've lost a black leather suitcase.
Ich glaube, ich habe ihn am Flughafen vergessen.	I think I left it at the airport.
In meinem Geldbeutel waren 100 Euro.	There were 100 euros in my wallet.
Haben Sie eine goldene Uhr gefunden?	Have you found a gold watch?
Könnten Sie sie mir zuschicken?	Could you post it to me?

ADVERTISING

◆ Foundation words

die Anzeige (n)	advert	hassen	to hate
ausverkauft	sold out	überrascht	surprised
die Ermäßigung (en)	reduction	unglaublich	unbelievable
das Sonderangebot (e)	special offer	einverstanden	agreed
die Werbung	publicity, advertising	der Blödsinn	nonsense
erstaunt	astonished	der Quatsch	nonsense

◆ Foundation phrases

Ich finde diese Werbung fabelhaft.	I find this advert fabulous.
Ich finde dieses Bild komisch.	I find this picture funny.
Ich finde dieses Foto wirklich hässlich.	I find this photo really ugly.
Die neuen CDs sind alle ausverkauft.	The new CDs have all been sold.
Diese Werbung ist Blödsinn.	This advert is rubbish.

◆ Higher words

die Reklame (n)	advert	der Slogan (s)	slogan
der Erfolg (e)	success	wirksam	effective
berühmt	famous	die Wahrheit	truth

◆ Higher phrases

Ich interessiere mich nicht für Werbung.	I'm not interested in advertising.

◆ Slogans

Match the slogans to the articles.

1 Ein Diamant ist unvergänglich

2 Vorsprung durch Technik

3 Ruf doch mal an

4 Katzen würden *Leckerbissen* essen

5 Was die Haut zum Leben braucht

6 Ein harter Tag braucht einen weichen Pullover

a) CLOTHES

b) JEWELLERY

c) COSMETICS

d) CARS

e) TELEPHONE

f) PET FOOD

(Answer on page 98)

41

MEDIA

◆ Foundation words

der Dokumentarfilm (e)	documentary	die Illustrierte (n)	magazine
fernsehen	to watch TV	die Zeitung (en)	newspaper
gucken	to watch, look	der Artikel (-)	article, item
das Radio (s)	radio		
die Presse	press		
die Zeitschrift (en)	magazine	*See page 52 for more about music and films.*	

◆ Foundation phrases

Was gibt es heute Abend im Fernsehen?	What's on television this evening?
Darf ich fernsehen?	May I watch television?
Letzten Samstag war ich im Kino.	I went to the cinema last Saturday.
Ich habe einen sehr guten Film gesehen.	I saw a very good film.
Hast du die neue Gruppe gehört?	Have you heard the new group?
Ich sehe sehr gern Krimis.	I really like watching thrillers.

◆ Higher words

raten	to advise	die Nachrichten (pl)	news
vorziehen	to prefer	die Tagesschau (sing.)	TV news
die Sendung (en)	programme	der Rundfunk	radio
umstritten	controversial		
		die Tageszeitung (en)	daily newspaper
das Satellitenbild (er)	satellite picture	die Wochenzeitung (en)	weekly newspaper
die Satellitenschüssel (n)	satellite dish	die Modezeitschrift (en)	fashion magazine
das Kabelfernsehen	cable TV		
die Serie (n)	series		
die Seifenoper (n)	soap (opera)	der Leser (-)	reader
die Folge (n)	episode	die Leserin (nen)	
die Reportage (n)	TV report	der Kommentar (e)	commentary
aktuell	current	das Abonnement (s)	subscription

MEDIA OPINIONS

◆ Foundation words

die Meinung (en)	opinion	komisch	funny
schlimm	awful	klasse	great
mies	awful	prima	terrific
ärgerlich	annoying	wunderbar	wonderful
langweilig	boring	Spitze	great
schlecht	bad	toll	terrific
doof	stupid	interessant	interesting
furchtbar	terrible	spannend	exciting
schwach	weak	super	super

◆ Higher words

hervorragend	outstanding	lächerlich	ridiculous
ekelhaft	disgusting	peinlich	embarrassing
entspannend	relaxing		

◆ Higher phrases

Ich halte nicht viel von diesem Film.	I don't think much of this film.
Diese Sendung kann ich empfehlen.	I can recommend this programme.
Der Schauspieler war klasse.	The actor was excellent.
Der Film hat mir nicht gefallen.	I didn't like the film.
Die Sendung war doof.	The programme was stupid.
Das ist die beste Sendung im Fernsehen.	That's the best programme on television.

HOW TO LEARN

VOCABULARY

When you have learned the words to do with a topic, copy them out with all the vowels missing. Then do something else for a while, and when you come back to the words, see if you can still fill in the vowels correctly.

What are these words?

1 d — r — nr — f = *phone call* ....

2 w — hl — n = *to dial* ....

3 b — s — tzt = *engaged* ....

4 d — r H — r — r = *receiver* ....

(Answer on page 98)

HOW TO USE A DICTIONARY

You need to practise finding a word in a dictionary as quickly as possible. Look at the first ten words in the **Lost Property Office** section on page 40. For each word, open your dictionary at the page where you guess the word will come. Then check the headwords at the top of the page to see how close you were. Then make another more accurate guess from the page you are already looking at. With practice, you will be able to find any word within a few seconds.

T I P P S ◆ T I P P S ◆ T I P P S ◆ T I P P S

Health and Welfare

◆ Foundation words

der Körper (-)	body	der Rücken (-)	back
der Kopf (¨e)	head	der Arm (e)	arm
das Auge (n)	eye	die Hand (¨e)	hand
der Mund (¨er)	mouth	der Finger (-)	finger
die Stimme (n)	voice	der Daumen (-)	thumb
die Nase (n)	nose	das Bein (e)	leg
das Ohr (en)	ear	der Fuß (¨e)	foot
der Zahn (¨e)	tooth	das Knie (-)	knee
der Hals (¨e)	neck, throat	brechen	to break
die Schulter (n)	shoulder	wehtun	to hurt
das Herz (en)	heart		
der Bauch (Bäuche)	stomach		
der Magen (-)	stomach	*See page 8 for describing appearance.*	

◆ Foundation phrases

Wo tut es weh?	Where does it hurt?
Mein Bein tut weh.	My leg hurts.
Ich habe Halsschmerzen.	I've got a sore throat.
Ich habe Bauchschmerzen.	I've got stomach ache.

◆ Higher words

die Zehe (n)	toe	die Niere (n)	kidney
der Knöchel (-)	ankle	die Stirn (en)	forehead
körperbehindert	physically disabled	die Brust (¨e)	chest, breast
		das Handgelenk (e)	wrist
das Blut	blood	das Fußgelenk (e)	ankle
die Leber (n)	liver	die Zunge (n)	tongue
die Lunge (n)	lung	die Haut (¨e)	skin

◆ Higher phrases

Er hat sich das Bein gebrochen.	He's broken his leg.
Ich habe mir den Knöchel verstaucht.	I've sprained my ankle.
Seit drei Tagen tut mein Arm weh.	My arm has been hurting for three days.

ILLNESS

◆ Foundation words

besser	better	die Allergie (n)	allergy
blass	pale	der Schnupfen (-)	cold
der Durst	thirst	erkältet sein	to have a cold
durstig	thirsty	sich erkälten	to catch a cold
der Hunger	hunger	der Heuschnupfen	hay fever
hungrig	hungry	atmen	to breathe
ernst	serious	atemlos	breathless
heiß	hot	husten	to cough
kalt	cold	das Fieber	temperature
müde	tired	die Grippe	flu
schwind(e)lig	dizzy		
übel	sick	die Schmerzen (pl)	pain
unfit	unfit	die Wunde (n)	wound
der Durchfall	diarrhoea	der Sonnenbrand	sunburn
		das Sonnenöl (e)	suntan oil
gesund	healthy	die Tube (n)	tube
krank	ill	die Sonnencreme (s)	suncream
die Krankheit (en)	illness		

◆ Foundation phrases

Geht es dir besser?	Do you feel better?
Es geht.	I'm alright.
Es geht mir nicht gut.	I don't feel well.
Was ist los?	What's wrong?
Ich bin krank.	I'm ill.
Mir ist kalt.	I feel cold.
Ich glaube, ich habe Fieber.	I think I've got a temperature.
Ich habe einen Schnupfen.	I've got a cold.
Ich habe eine schlimme Erkältung.	I've got a bad cold.

◆ Higher words

die Masern (pl)	measles	verstopft	constipated
schwitzen	to sweat	allergisch gegen	allergic to
der Sonnenstich	sunstroke	betrunken	drunk
seekrank	sea-sick	der Insektenstich (e)	insect bite
weinen	to cry	der Wespenstich (e)	wasp sting
niesen	to sneeze	stechen	to sting
bluten	to bleed	der Puls (e)	pulse
bewegen	to move	die Verletzung (en)	injury
sich erbrechen	to vomit	der Krebs	cancer

AIDS	AIDS	taub	deaf
		die Kraft (¨e)	strength
der Stress (e)	stress	die Stimme (n)	voice
der Alptraum (-träume)	nightmare	die Füllung (en)	filling
atmen	to breathe	leiden an	to suffer from
schlucken	to swallow		

◆ **Higher phrases**

Ich habe mich zweimal erbrochen.	I've been sick twice.
Er hat sich die Hand verbrannt.	He's burnt his hand.
Ich habe mich in den Finger geschnitten.	I've cut my finger.
Er ist schwer verletzt.	He's seriously injured.
Ich leide an Heuschnupfen.	I suffer from hay fever.

RECOVERY AND EMERGENCY

◆ **Foundation words**

die Hilfe	help	der Verband (¨e)	bandage
die Apotheke (n)	(dispensing) chemist's	die Besserung	recovery
		einreiben	to rub in
der Arzt (¨e)	doctor	das Pflaster (-)	plaster
die Ärztin (nen)		das Medikament (e)	medicine (drug)
die Klinik (en)	clinic		
der Krankenwagen (-)	ambulance	die Medizin	medicine (science)
das Krankenhaus (-häuser)	hospital		
der Krankenpfleger (-)	nurse	operieren	to operate
die Krankenschwester (n)		die Pille (n)	pill
der Zahnarzt (-ärzte)	dentist	die Tablette (n)	tablet
die Zahnärztin (nen)		untersuchen	to examine
die Sprechstunde (n)	surgery time	verschreiben	to prescribe

Who would visit these people?

Zahnärztlicher Notdienst
Illertissen/Vöhringen/Weißenhorn/
Senden/Dietenheim/Illerrieden:
10–12, 18–19 Uhr, Dr. Weckerle,
Weißenhorn, Bahnhofstraße 14,
Telefon Praxis (07309) 30 15;
Wohnung (07309) 30 16.

Dr. med. H. Rolfs
Arzt f. Kinderheilkunde
Tel. 54982
Mo.–Fr. 8–12 u. 15–18 Uhr
und nach Vereinbarung
Außer Mittwochnachmittag

der Unfall (-fälle)	accident	schneiden	to cut
die Gefahr (en)	danger	sterben	to die
die Lebensgefahr	mortal danger	verletzen	to injure
der Brand ("e)	fire		
das Feuer (-)	fire	abnehmen	to lose weight
der Feuerlöscher (-)	fire extinguisher	zunehmen	to put on weight
die Feuerwehr (en)	fire brigade	die erste Hilfe	first aid
der Feuerwehrwagen (-)	fire engine	der Erste-Hilfe-Kasten (-Kästen)	first aid box
das Leben (-)	life	die Kopfschmerz-tablette (n)	headache tablet
der Notdienst (e)	emergency service	schützen	to protect
der Notfall (-fälle)	emergency	sicher	safe
dringend	urgent		

◆ Foundation phrases

Haben Sie etwas gegen Sonnenbrand?	Have you got something for sunburn?
Ich brauche einen Zahnarzt.	I need a dentist.
Können Sie mir etwas verschreiben?	Can you prescribe something for me?
Ich muss im Bett bleiben.	I must stay in bed.
Er sollte eine Diät machen.	He should go on a diet.

◆ Higher words

sich erholen	to recover	der Rettungsdienst (e)	rescue service
der Gips (e)	plastercast	der Rettungswagen (-)	ambulance
die Salbe (n)	ointment	die Versicherung (en)	insurance
die Praxis (Praxen)	doctor's surgery	die Krankenkasse (n)	medical insurance
röntgen	to X-ray	der Rollstuhl (-stühle)	wheelchair
das Röntgenbild (er)	X-ray	pflegen	to look after
der Blutdruck	blood pressure	die Verbesserung (en)	improvement
die Blutprobe (n)	blood test	einen Termin machen	to make an appointment
schwach	weak		
erschöpft	exhausted		
die Untersuchung (en)	check-up	die Gesundheit	health
die Behandlung (en)	treatment	die Diät (en)	weight-loss diet
behandeln	to treat	die Figur (en)	figure
der Rettungsschwimmer (-) die Rettungsschwimmerin (nen)	lifeguard		

◆ **Higher phrases**

Ich möchte mich eine Weile hinlegen.	I'd like to lie down for a while.
Ich muss ein paar Kilo abnehmen.	I must lose a few kilos.
Sie ist bei guter Gesundheit.	She's in good health.
Sie hatte den Arm in Gips.	She had her arm in plaster.

HEALTHY LIVING

◆ **Foundation words**

das Essen (-)	food, meal	der Schaden (¨)	harm
essen	to eat	die Gefahr (en)	danger
das Getränk (e)	drink	gefährlich	dangerous
trinken	to drink	der Alkohol	alcohol
gesund	healthy, healthily	alkoholfrei	alcohol-free
		der Rauch	smoke
ungesund	unhealthy, unhealthily	rauchen	to smoke
		die Zigarette (n)	cigarette
die Mahlzeit (en)	meal	der Tabak (e)	tobacco
der Sport (sing.)	sport, exercise	die Droge (n)	drug
Sport treiben	to exercise	Drogen nehmen	to take drugs

◆ **Foundation phrases**

Ich rauche nicht. Es ist schlecht für die Gesundheit.	I don't smoke. It's bad for your health.
Ich treibe viel Sport, zum Beispiel…	I do a lot of exercise, for example…

◆ **Higher words**

das Aerobic	aerobics	das Fastfood	fast food
der Heimtrainer (-)	exercise bike, exercise machine	der Alkoholiker (-) die Alkoholikerin (nen)	alcoholic
der Fitnesskurs (e)	fitness class	der Alkoholismus	alcoholism
das Jogging	jogging	der Raucher (-) die Raucherin (nen)	smoker
fit	fit		
fit bleiben	to keep fit	passives Rauchen	passive smoking
		das Rauchen aufgeben	to stop smoking
die Lebensmittel (pl)	food	das Risiko (-ken)	risk
fettarm	low-fat	das Gesundheitsrisiko (-ken)	health risk
fettig	fatty		

48

◆ **Higher phrases**

Ich esse keine Schokolade, weil sie dick macht.	I don't eat chocolate because it's fattening.
Ich habe letztes Jahr das Rauchen aufgegeben.	I stopped smoking last year.
Ich tue mein Bestes, um fit zu bleiben.	I do my best to keep fit.
Ich gehe dreimal in der Woche zum Aerobickurs.	I go to aerobics classes three times a week.
Meiner Meinung nach ist es sehr gefährlich, Drogen zu nehmen.	In my opinion, taking drugs is very dangerous.
fettiges Essen essen	to eat fatty food

HOW TO LEARN

VOCABULARY

German likes to make long words by joining together two or more short ones. For example, *Blutdruck* is just *Blut* (blood) and *Druck* (pressure) joined together. The gender of the new word is always the same as the gender of the last word, so it is *der Blutdruck* because it is *der Druck*. Once you are used to breaking down German words in this way, they are not as frightening as they first seem.

What do these three long words mean? (They have been split to help you.)

1 die Kopf/wunde   ....

2 der Not/ausgang   ....

3 die Lebens/gefahr   ....

(Answer on page 98)

HOW TO USE A DICTIONARY

As in all languages, some words in German have more than one meaning. (The word *der Zug* is famous for the number of different meanings it has!) In your dictionary look up these four words from this section to find meanings other than the ones given:

1 der Brand   ....

2 verschreiben   ....

3 das Pflaster   ....

4 die Stimme   ....

(Answer on page 98)

TIPPS ◆ TIPPS ◆ TIPPS ◆ TIPPS ◆ TIPPS ◆ TIPPS ◆

49

Free Time

HOBBIES AND SPORT

◆ **Foundation words**

sich interessieren für	to be interested in	rennen	to run
sich amüsieren	to enjoy oneself	spazieren gehen	to go walking
das Hobby (s)	hobby	der Spaziergang (-gänge)	walk
die Freizeit	free time	wandern	to hike
der Feierabend (e)	free time after work	die Wanderung (en)	hike
die Freizeit- beschäftigung (en)	leisure activity	das Bergsteigen	mountain climbing
das Interesse (n)	interest	klettern	to climb
der Anfänger (-) die Anfängerin (nen)	beginner	Ski fahren	to ski
		Rad fahren	to cycle
		reiten	to ride
das Dia (s)	slide	der Rollschuh (e)	rollerskate
das Foto (s)	photo	der Schlittschuh (e)	ice skate
der Fotoapparat (e)	camera	das Sportzentrum (-zentren)	sports centre
fotografieren	to take a photo	das Fitnesszentrum (-zentren)	fitness centre
basteln	to make things	die Gymnastik	keep-fit
nähen	to sew	schwimmen	to swim
sammeln	to collect	das Schwimmbad (¨er)	swimming pool
zeichnen	to draw	das Freibad (¨er)	open-air pool
der Aufkleber (-)	sticker	das Hallenbad (-bäder)	indoor pool
die Puppe (n)	doll	rudern	to row
das Spielzeug (e)	toy(s)	segeln	to sail
der Horrorroman (e)	horror story		
der Liebesroman (e)	love story	das Tennis	tennis
der Kriminalroman (e)	detective story	das Tischtennis	table tennis
das Schach	chess	das Badminton	badminton
		der Federball	badminton
Sport treiben	to do sports	der Schläger (-)	bat, racquet
die Sportart (en)	kind of sport	werfen	to throw
der Sportler (-) die Sportlerin (nen)	sports person	kegeln	to go bowling
der Verein (e)	club	die Kegelbahn (en)	bowling alley
		der Fußball	football
angeln	to fish	spielen	to play
die Angelrute (n)	fishing rod	das Spiel (e)	game, match
fischen	to fish	das Endspiel (e)	final
joggen	to jog	gewinnen	to win

verlieren	to lose	der Fan (s)	fan
der Sportverein (e)	sports club	der Zuschauer (-)	spectator
der Sportplatz (-plätze)	sports field	die Zuschauerin (nen)	
das Stadion (Stadien)	stadium		
die Mannschaft (en)	team	der Freizeitpark (s)	theme park

◆ **Foundation phrases**

Ich habe nicht viel Freizeit.	I don't have a lot of free time.
Ich fahre sehr gern Ski.	I like skiing.
Jedes Wochenende gehe ich angeln.	I go fishing every weekend.
Letzten Samstag habe ich Tischtennis gespielt.	Last Saturday I played table tennis.
Gestern bin ich spazieren gegangen.	I went for a walk yesterday.
Am Wochenende gehe ich ins Hallenbad.	I go to the swimming pool at the weekends.
Wir freuen uns auf das Spiel.	We're looking forward to the match.
Ich spiele nicht gern Tennis.	I don't like playing tennis.
Das Spiel endet um siebzehn Uhr.	The match finishes at five o'clock.
Tennis macht Spaß.	Tennis is fun.

◆ **Higher words**

der Pfadfinder (-)	boy scout	der Pokal (e)	cup
die Pfadfinderin (nen)	girl guide	das Unentschieden (-)	draw
die Sammlung (en)	collection	fangen	to catch
rätseln	to do puzzles	trainieren	to train
		sich trimmen	to keep fit
sich entspannen	to relax	das Ausdauertraining (-)	endurance training
die Unterhaltung	entertainment		
geschickt	skilful	die Kampfsportart (en)	martial art
ein Tor schießen	to score a goal	das Mountainbike (s)	mountain bike
das Turnier (e)	tournament	das Kanu (s)	canoe
der Wettbewerb (e)	competition	das Brettspiel (e)	board game
die Meisterschaft (en)	championship		

◆ **Higher phrases**

Ich war früher Pfadfinder.	I used to be a scout.
Ich trainiere dreimal die Woche.	I train three times a week.
Ich bin in Höchstform.	I'm on top form.

FREE TIME

◆ **Hobbies**

Write the German hobby for these 6 pictures in your order of preference, starting with your favourite one.

1 ....
2 ....
3 ....
4 ....
5 ....
6 ....

MUSIC AND FILMS

◆ **Foundation words**

die Band (s)	band
der Sänger (-)	singer
die Sängerin (nen)	
die Gruppe (n)	group
die CD (s)	CD
die Stereoanlage (n)	stereo
die Platte (n)	record
die Schallplatte (n)	record
die Kassette (n)	cassette
der Walkman (s)	walkman
hören	to hear
singen	to sing
das Lied (er)	song
die Diskothek (en)	discotheque
tanzen	to dance
die Oper (n)	opera
das Orchester (-)	orchestra
das Konzert (e)	concert
der Chor (¨e)	choir
das Instrument (e)	instrument
die Blockflöte (n)	recorder
die Gitarre (n)	guitar
die Geige (n)	violin
das Schlagzeug (e)	drums
die Trompete (n)	trumpet
das Kino (s)	cinema
der Film (e)	film

der Trickfilm (e)	cartoon
der Krimi (s)	thriller
die Nachrichten (pl)	news
das Programm (e)	schedule, channel
die Sendung (en)	programme
der Schauspieler (-)	actor
die Schauspielerin (nen)	actress
anschauen	to look at
das Theater (-)	theatre
das Theaterstück (e)	play
das Parkett (e)	stalls
das Parterre (-)	rear stalls
der Rang (¨e)	circle
die Vorstellung (en)	performance
die Karte (n)	ticket
die Kasse (n)	ticket office
die Ermäßigung (en)	reduction
kaufen	to buy
der Eintritt	entrance
das Eintrittsgeld (er)	entrance fee
der Preis (e)	price
anfangen	to begin
enden	to end

See page 42 for more about the media.

52

◆ **Foundation phrases**

Ich interessiere mich für Musik.	I'm interested in music.
Ich singe im Chor.	I sing in the choir.
Wann beginnt/endet der Film?	When does the film start/finish?
Was kostet eine Karte, bitte?	What does a ticket cost, please?
Zweimal, bitte.	Two tickets, please
Was läuft?	What's on?
Was für ein Konzert ist es?	What sort of concert is it?
Gibt es einen Sonderpreis für Studenten?	Is there a special price for students?
Es war wirklich klasse/mies.	It was really great/awful.
Ich fand das Konzert langweilig.	I found the concert boring.
Der Film war echt spannend.	The film was really exciting.

◆ **Higher words**

die Blaskapelle (n)	brass band	die Aufführung (en)	performance
das Ballett (e)	ballet	das Schauspiel (e)	play
musizieren	to make music	der Held (en)	hero
die Bühne (n)	stage	die Heldin (nen)	heroine
der Komponist (en)	composer	der Bösewicht (e)	baddie
die Komponistin (nen)		die Figur (en)	character
synchronisiert	dubbed	die Tragödie (n)	tragedy
aufführen	to stage, perform	der Abenteuerfilm (e)	adventure film

◆ **Higher phrases**

Ich bin Mitglied in einer Blaskapelle.	I'm a member of a brass band.
Klavierspielen macht Spaß.	Playing the piano is fun.

TRIPS AND MEETINGS

◆ **Foundation words**

der Ausflug (-flüge)	excursion	der Jugendklub (s)	youth club
der Besuch (e)	visit	das Museum (Museen)	museum
die Fahrt (en)	journey	der Zoo (s)	zoo
die Rundfahrt (en)	round trip		
ausgehen	to go out	abgemacht	agreed
		in Ordnung	alright
einladen	to invite	die Idee (n)	idea
die Einladung (en)	invitation	nett	nice
frei	free	treffen	to meet
beschäftigt	busy	begeistert	enthusiastic
		Lust haben	to want to
die Galerie (n)	gallery		

◆ Foundation phrases

Was machst du heute Abend?	What are you doing this evening?
Hast du Lust, ins Kino zu gehen?	Do you want to go to the cinema?
Möchtest du ins Konzert gehen?	Would you like to go to the concert?
Kommst du mit?	Do you want to come with me/us?
Wann/Wo treffen wir uns?	When/Where are we going to meet?
Vielen Dank für die Einladung.	Thank you very much for the invitation.
Ich möchte lieber in die Diskothek gehen.	I'd prefer to go to the discotheque.
Wann hat das Schwimmbad auf?	When does the swimming pool open?
Ich kann nicht zum Spiel kommen.	I can't come to the match.

◆ Higher words

besorgen	to obtain	die Gelegenheit (en)	opportunity

◆ Higher phrases

Wie wäre es mit einem Theaterstück?	How about a play?
Ich ziehe Komödien vor.	I prefer comedies.

◆ Film titles

What are these films called in English?

1	**Der König der Löwen**
2	**Ein Schweinchen namens Babe**
3	**Leben und sterben lassen**
4	**Dschungelbuch**
5	**Vier Hochzeiten und ein Todesfall**
6	**Sinn und Sinnlichkeit**

(Answer on page 98)

HOW TO LEARN

VOCABULARY

If this book belongs to you, highlight words that apply to you or tick words that you have learned; then add other words that apply to you. You could do this in the **Notes** section on page 100. Customise your vocabulary so that you can talk about what interests and concerns you personally.

HOW TO USE A DICTIONARY

Your dictionary should have a list of verbs in it with all the perfect and imperfect tenses of irregular verbs. Make sure that you know where it is and how to use it to help you with homework and coursework.

Use your dictionary verb list to find out the perfect tense of these four verbs:

ich schwimme	–	ich bin geschwommen	
1 ich gewinne	–	ich habe	....
2 ich reite	–	ich bin	....
3 ich treffe	–	ich habe	....
4 ich singe	–	ich habe	....

(Answer on page 98)

Social Activities

SOCIALISING

◆ Foundation words

guten Morgen	good morning	der Glückwunsch ("e)	congratulations
guten Tag	hello	alles Gute	all the best
guten Abend	good evening	viel Spaß	have fun
gute Nacht	good night	viel Glück	good luck
grüß dich	hello	gute Reise	safe journey
hallo	hello	Vorsicht	careful
auf Wiedersehen	goodbye		
tschüs	bye	der Heiligabend	Christmas Eve
auf Wiederhören	bye (on phone)	das Weihnachten	Christmas
servus	hello/goodbye	der Silvester(abend)	New Year's Eve
bis später	see you later	das Neujahr	New Year's Day
bis bald	see you soon	der Fasching	carnival (South)
		der Karneval	carnival (North)
begrüßen	to greet	der Aschermittwoch	Ash Wednesday
willkommen	welcome	das Ostern	Easter
hereinkommen	to come in	der erste Januar	January 1st
sich setzen	to sit down		
danke	thank you	das Fest (e)	party
nichts zu danken	don't mention it	stattfinden	to take place
dankbar	grateful	feiern	to celebrate
hoffen	to hope		
winken	to wave		

See page 53 for more about trips.

◆ Foundation phrases

Willkommen in England!	Welcome to England!
Es freut mich, Sie kennen zu lernen.	Pleased to meet you.
Ich habe nichts dagegen.	I've nothing against that.
Es kommt darauf an.	It depends.
Es macht nichts.	It doesn't matter.
Es tut mir Leid.	I'm sorry.
Herzlichen Glückwunsch zum Geburtstag!	Happy birthday!
Ich finde Weihnachten so schön.	I like Christmas so much.
Am Heiligabend gehen wir in die Kirche.	We go to church on Christmas Eve.
Ich schicke viele Weihnachtskarten.	I send lots of Christmas cards.
Wir bekommen Geschenke.	We get presents.
Es grüßt dich herzlich…	Regards from…
Fröhliche Weihnachten!	Merry Christmas!
Frohe Ostern!	Happy Easter!

◆ Higher words

einverstanden	agreed	der Advents-kalender (-)	Advent calendar
Verzeihung	sorry	der Adventskranz (-kränze)	Advent wreath
sich duzen	to use the "du" form	die Bescherung (en)	giving of Christmas presents
sich siezen	to use the "Sie" form	die Fastenzeit (-)	Lent
sich entschuldigen	to apologise	der Karfreitag (e)	Good Friday
gleichfalls	the same to you	die Kirchweih (en)	fair
der Umzug (-züge)	procession	die Kirmes (-)	fair
das Feuerwerk (e)	fireworks (display)	das Gedränge (-)	crowd
die Kerze (n)	candle	ablehnen	to turn down

◆ Higher phrases

Ich gratuliere! — Congratulations!
Ich werde mich verabschieden. — I'll take my leave.
Hoffentlich wird es klappen. — I hope it'll turn out OK.

SOCIAL ACTIVITIES

◆ Foundation words

die Ausstellung (en)	exhibition	die Gastfreundschaft	hospitality
der Feiertag (e)	festival, day off	der Gastgeber (-)	host
		die Gastgeberin (-nen)	hostess
der Bekannte (n)	acquaintance	vorstellen	to introduce
die Bekannte (n)		treffen	to meet
der Freund (e)	friend	begegnen	to meet
die Freundin (nen)		begleiten	to accompany
freundlich	friendly		
befreundet sein	to be friends	die Weinprobe (n)	wine tasting
der Brieffreund (e)	penfriend	die Weinstube (n)	wine bar
die Brieffreundin (nen)		die Weintraube (n)	grape
die Brieffreundschaft (en)	penfriendship	die Bierhalle (n)	beer hall
der Gast (¨e)	guest	zum Wohl	cheers

◆ Foundation phrases

Wo treffen wir uns? — Where shall we meet?
Darf ich meine Mutter vorstellen? — May I introduce my mother?
Hier ist mein Bruder. — This is my brother.
Hoffentlich hast du eine gute Reise gehabt. — I hope you've had a good journey.
Was möchtest du machen? — What would you like to do?

Hier ist dein Schlafzimmer.	This is your bedroom.
Vielen Dank für Ihre Gastfreundschaft.	Thank you very much for your hospitality.
Es war sehr schön.	It was lovely.
Hoffentlich kommst du bald zu uns.	I hope you'll come to see us soon.

◆ Higher words

die Gastfamilie (n)	host family		das Vergnügen (-)	pleasure
sich verabreden	to arrange to meet		zufrieden	satisfied
die Stimmung	atmosphere		kontaktfreudig	sociable
sich bedanken	to say thank you			

◆ Higher phrases

Möchtest du das Badezimmer benutzen?	Would you like to use the bathroom?
Du kannst dich frisch machen.	You can refresh yourself.
Es war mir ein Vergnügen.	The pleasure was mine.
Ausgeschlafen?	Have you slept well?
Komm gut nach Hause.	Have a safe journey home.

HOW TO LEARN

VOCABULARY

A simple way to test yourself quickly on words you have learned is to chop them in half and write them down in two lists. Later you try to put the words back together again. Put these chopped-up words back together again:

Gast	stellen	....
beg	tag	....
vor	geber	....
ab	inde	....
Feier	lehnen	....
Geme	egnen	....

(Answer on page 98)

HOW TO USE A DICTIONARY

Set phrases are often difficult to translate, because you don't translate them word for word. If you want to say "it doesn't matter" and you look up "matter", don't end up choosing the wrong word. The dictionary will usually give you the whole phrase. Look up the underlined words in a dictionary to see if the whole phrase is given.

1 Happy birthday!

2 You're welcome!

3 Bad luck!

Tourism

HOLIDAYS

◆ **Foundation words**

die Ferien (pl)	holidays	der Luxus	luxury
der Urlaub (e)	holiday	der Reisebus (se)	touring coach
bleiben	to stay	die Grenze (n)	border
im Ausland	abroad	der Zoll (¨e)	customs
im Inland	at home (not abroad)	die Zollkontrolle (n)	customs check
		der Pass (¨e)	passport
sich freuen auf	to look forward to	erreichen	to reach
planen	to plan	der Reisende (n)	traveller
das Reisebüro (s)	travel agent's	die Reisende (n)	
die Broschüre (n)	brochure	besichtigen	to visit, view
reisen	to travel	der Führer (-)	guide book
die Reise (n)	journey	die Stadtführung (en)	guided tour
der Tourist (en)	tourist	zeigen	to show
die Touristin (nen)			
das Ziel (e)	destination	der Strand (¨e)	beach
fremd	strange, foreign	der See (n)	lake
das Heimweh	home sickness	die See (n)	sea
		an der See	by the sea
packen	to pack	an der Küste	on the coast
einpacken	to pack	der Spielplatz (¨e)	play area
auspacken	to unpack	sich sonnen	to sunbathe
der Ausweis (e)	ID card		
der Koffer (-)	suitcase	das Informationsbüro (s)	information office
das Gepäck	luggage	die Sehenswürdigkeiten (pl)	sights
der Aufenthalt (e)	stay		
die Heimfahrt (en)	journey home		

◆ **Foundation phrases**

Ich freue mich auf die Ferien.	I'm looking forward to the holidays.
Wir fahren oft ins Ausland.	We often go abroad.
Ich fahre mit meinen Eltern in Urlaub.	I go on holiday with my parents.
Zu Ostern waren wir in der Schweiz.	We went to Switzerland at Easter.
Wir waren zwei Wochen dort.	We were there for two weeks.
Wir haben viele Ausflüge gemacht.	We went on lots of excursions.
Wir sind oft Rad gefahren.	We often went cycling.
Wir sind jeden Tag schwimmen gegangen.	We went swimming every day.
Ich war mit meinen Eltern im Ausland.	I went abroad with my parents.
Wir waren jeden Tag am Strand.	We went to the beach every day.

TOURISM

◆ Higher words

die Unterkunft (-künfte)	accommodation
Unterkunft und Verpflegung	board and lodgings
unterbringen	to accommodate
die Ferienwohnung (en)	holiday home
die Pauschalreise (n)	package holiday
der Urlauber (-) die Urlauberin (nen)	holiday maker
der Reiseleiter (-) die Reiseleiterin (nen)	courier
der Kurort (e)	spa town
abreisen	to leave, set off
herumreisen	to travel around
der Mietwagen (-)	hire car
die Aufnahme (n)	photo
knipsen	to take pictures
die Seilbahn (en)	cable car
die Sesselbahn (en)	chair lift
die Veranstaltung (en)	event
surfen	to surf
tauchen	to dive
faulenzen	to laze around
berühmt	famous
hervorragend	outstanding
sehenswert	worth seeing

◆ Higher phrases

Man kann da viel unternehmen.	You can do a lot there.
Ich habe vor, ins Ausland zu fahren.	I intend to go abroad.
Köln ist eine Reise wert.	Cologne is worth a visit.
Wir haben viele Aufnahmen gemacht.	We took lots of photos.

HOTELS AND YOUTH HOSTELS

◆ Foundation words

das Hotel (s)	hotel
die Pension (en)	small hotel
die Jugendherberge (n)	youth hostel
das Hotelverzeichnis (se)	list of hotels
mieten	to rent, hire
reservieren	to reserve
buchen	to book
die Vollpension	full board
die Halbpension	half board
das Zimmer (-)	room
das Einzelzimmer (-)	single room
das Doppelzimmer (-)	double room
das Familienzimmer (-)	family room
das Fremdenzimmer (-)	guest room
der Platz ("e)	space
die Reservierung (en)	reservation
der Saal (Säle)	hall
der Schlüssel (-)	key
die Rechnung (en)	bill
der Balkon (e)	balcony
der Blick (e)	view
möbliert	furnished
der Lift (e)	lift
der Aufzug (-züge)	lift
der Fahrstuhl (-stühle)	lift
der Herbergsvater (") die Herbergsmutter (")	warden
der Empfangschef (s) die Empfangsdame (n)	receptionist
der Portier (s)	porter
das Zimmermädchen (-)	chamber maid
übernachten	to spend the night
die Übernachtung (en)	overnight stay

◆ Foundation phrases

Haben Sie ein Zimmer für heute Abend?	Have you got a room for tonight?
Haben Sie noch zwei Zimmer frei?	Have you got two rooms free?
Ich möchte ein Einzelzimmer mit Dusche.	I'd like a single room with a shower.
Ich habe ein Zimmer mit Bad reserviert.	I've reserved a room with a bath.
Was kostet es pro Person?	What does it cost per person?
Was kostet ein Zimmer mit Bad?	What does a room with a bath cost?
Was kostet Vollpension?	What does full board cost?
Es ist mir zu teuer.	It's too expensive for me.
Haben Sie etwas Billigeres?	Have you got anything cheaper?
Ich nehme das Zimmer.	I'll take the room.
Wir sind zwei Mädchen und ein Junge.	There are two girls and a boy.
Wann ist Frühstück?	When is breakfast?
Ich hätte gern die Rechnung, bitte.	I'd like the bill, please.
Was kostet eine Übernachtung?	What does a night's stay cost?

A model letter to a hotel:

An die Hotelleitung
Hotel am See
Mozartstraße 23
61352 Bad Homburg am See

16. Juni 2002

Sehr geehrte Damen und Herren,

ich möchte vom 9. bis zum 18. August ein Doppelzimmer mit Bad und auch ein Einzelzimmer mit Dusche reservieren. Wir möchten nur Frühstück.

Könnten Sie mir bitte Informationen über die Einrichtungen im Hotel und eine Preisliste schicken? Gibt es auch ein Hallenbad im Hotel?

Meine Adresse ist:

Ich danke Ihnen im Voraus.

Mit freundlichen Grüßen

…

◆ Higher words

die Einrichtungen (pl)	facilities	der Pförtner (-)	porter
ausfüllen	to fill in	die Pförtnerin (nen)	
die Mehrwertsteuer	VAT	die Aussicht	view
die Bedienung	service	die Tiefgarage (n)	underground
inklusive	inclusive		car park
sich beschweren	to complain	der Tagesraum (-räume)	dayroom
sich beklagen	to complain	die Hausordnung (en)	house rules
unerhört	disgraceful		

◆ Higher phrases

Ich wollte ein Zimmer mit Aussicht.	I wanted a room with a view.
Ich möchte mich beim Manager beschweren.	I want to complain to the manager.
Leider habe ich die Dusche kaputtgemacht.	Unfortunately I've broken the shower.

Read these two adverts.

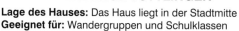

Hotel »Zur Alpenrose«
Familie Dr. Kathrein
**6433 Oetz – Hauptstraße 39,
Telefon 62 08**

Erholung und Gemütlichkeit finden Sie im Hotel »Zur Alpenrose« in Oetz. Die anerkannt gute internationale Küche und ein sehenswerter Speisesaal zählen zu den Vorzügen des Hauses. Alle Zimmer mit Dusche und WC, geheiztes Freischwimmbad – Liegewiese

 JUGENDHERBERGE TUTTLINGEN

Lage des Hauses: Das Haus liegt in der Stadtmitte
Geeignet für: Wandergruppen und Schulklassen

Freizeitangebot: Ausflüge: Bodensee 30 km, Schwarzwald 25 km, Schwäbische Alb und Donautal, Ausflugskarten in die Schweiz und Österreich
Bankverbindung: Kreissparkasse Tuttlingen, BLZ 643 500 70, Konto 40 606
Nächste Jugendherbergen: Rottweil 30 km, Singen 30 km, Villingen 35 km, Burg Wildenstein 25 km
Wichtiger Hinweis: Die Jugendherberge ist vom 1.10. bis 1.04. geschlossen

C A M P I N G

◆ Foundation words

das Zelt (e)	tent	der Rucksack (-säcke)	rucksack
zelten	to camp	der Schlafsack (-säcke)	sleeping bag
der Campingplatz (-plätze)	campsite	das Streichholz ("er)	match
der Wohnwagen (-)	caravan	trinkbar	drinkable
der Campingkocher (-)	camp stove	untrinkbar	undrinkable
der Dosenöffner (-)	tin opener		

◆ Foundation phrases

Was kostet es für eine Nacht für ein Zelt?	What does it cost for one night for a tent?
Haben Sie noch Platz für einen Wohnwagen?	Do you still have space for a caravan?
Gibt es einen Spielplatz?	Is there a play area?
Das Wasser hier ist untrinkbar.	The water here is not for drinking.

◆ Higher words

das Lagerfeuer (-)	camp fire	die Luftmatratze (n)	airbed
der Strom	electric current	der Schatten (-)	shade
der Abfall (Abfälle)	rubbish	der Klappstuhl (-stühle)	folding chair
die Nachtruhe	lights out	das Wohnmobil (e)	dormobile
die Gebühr (en)	fee		

◆ Higher phrases

Kann man eine Luftmatratze ausleihen?	Can you hire an air bed?
Wo sollen wir unser Zelt aufschlagen?	Where should we pitch our tent?
Sind Lagerfeuer erlaubt?	Are camp fires allowed?
Ich hätte lieber einen Platz im Schatten.	I'd prefer a place in the shade.

Read these campsite notices.

Rauchen verboten

ROLLSTUHLGERECHT

CAMPINGPLATZ
im Erholungs- und Freizeitpark
"Auf der Lach" – direkt am Rhein
Geöffnet von 15. Mai bis 15. September

CAMPINGPLATZ
beim Ponyhof "Landgut Ebental"
Geöffnet von April bis Oktober

Ihren Abfall geben Sie bitte in die Abfalleimer und Glas bringen Sie natürlich nicht mit!

TRINKWASSER

HOW TO LEARN

VOCABULARY

If you like using computers and you have one at home, set up your own vocabulary database, which you can regularly update. This can be by topic, alphabetical, German–English or English–German, or whatever you choose. Set yourself little tests and games on the computer, which you can save and use for revision later. You could, for example, write out some key phrases with words missing, which you have below, and which you need to cut and paste to complete the sentences. Your screen might look like the one here.

---

1. Wir kommen - - - siebzehn - - - an.

2. Das - - - ist am Montag - - -

3. Was - - - es für eine Nacht
   für ein - - - ?

   Restaurant, Zelt, gegen, kostet,
   geschlossen, Uhr

HOW TO USE A DICTIONARY

Your dictionary helps not just with meaning but also with spellings. Use your dictionary to correct the spellings of the underlined words in these sentences:

1 Wir brauchen ein <u>Streicholz</u> für das Feuer.   ....

2 Ich habe meinen <u>Schussel</u> verloren.   ....

3 Ich möchte die Stadt <u>beschigtigen</u>.   ....

(Answer on page 98)

International World

THE WIDER WORLD

◆ **Foundation words**

Europa	Europe
die EU	EU
Afrika	Africa
Amerika	America
die USA	USA
Asien	Asia
Großbritannien	Great Britain
England	England
Schottland	Scotland
Irland	Ireland
Wales	Wales
die Bundesländer (pl)	federal states
Deutschland	Germany
Österreich	Austria
die Schweiz	Switzerland
Belgien	Belgium
Holland	Holland
die Niederlande (pl)	Netherlands
Dänemark	Denmark
Norwegen	Norway
Schweden	Sweden
Frankreich	France
Spanien	Spain
Griechenland	Greece
Italien	Italy
die Türkei	Turkey
Polen	Poland
Rumänien	Rumania
Russland	Russia
die Slowakei	Slovakia
Ungarn	Hungary
der Ausländer (-)	foreigner
die Ausländerin (nen)	
der Amerikaner (-)	American
die Amerikanerin (nen)	
der Brite (n)	Briton
die Britin (nen)	
der Deutsche (n)	German
die Deutsche (n)	

der Franzose (n)	Frenchman
die Französin (nen)	Frenchwoman
der Holländer (-)	Dutchman
die Holländerin (nen)	Dutchwoman
der Italiener (-)	Italian
die Italienerin (nen)	
der Österreicher (-)	Austrian
die Österreicherin (nen)	
der Schweizer (-)	Swiss
die Schweizerin (nen)	
der Spanier (-)	Spaniard
die Spanierin (nen)	
der Waliser (-)	Welshman
die Waliserin (nen)	Welshwoman
walisisch	Welsh
Wien	Vienna
Bayern	Bavaria
Köln	Cologne
München	Munich
die Alpen (pl)	Alps
der Bodensee	Lake Constance
die Ostsee	Baltic
die Nordsee	North Sea
das Mittelmeer	Mediterranean
der Rhein	Rhine
die Donau	Danube
die Themse	Thames
der Osten	East
der Norden	North
der Westen	West
der Süden	South
die Mark (-)	mark
der Euro (-)	euro
der Euroschein (e)	euro note
gratis, kostenlos	free
sich anmelden	to register
der Anmeldezettel (-)	registration papers

65

◆ Foundation phrases

Ich war in der Türkei.	I was in Turkey.
Meine Großeltern wohnen in Frankreich.	My grandparents live in France.
Warst du je in Russland?	Have you ever been to Russia?
Mein Vater ist Holländer.	My father is Dutch.
Was kostet es?	What does it cost?
Das kostet zwanzig Euro.	That costs twenty euros.

◆ Higher words

die Politik (sing.)	politics	der König (e)	king
der Politiker (-)	politician	die Königin (nen)	queen
die Politikerin (nen)		die Vereinigten	United States
der Präsident (en)	president	Staaten (pl)	
die Präsidentin (nen)			
der Bundeskanzler (-)	German		
die Bundeskanzlerin (nen)	chancellor		

◆ Higher phrases

die ehemalige DDR	former East Germany

SOCIAL ISSUES

◆ Foundation words

der Verbrecher (-)	criminal	die Ursache (n)	cause
die Verbrecherin (nen)		die Hoffnung (en)	hope
der Taschendieb (e)	pick-pocket	der Hunger	hunger
die Taschendiebin (nen)		der Krieg (e)	war
der Diebstahl (¨e)	theft	die Möglichkeit (en)	possibility
der Dieb (e)	thief	die Not (¨e)	emergency
die Diebin (nen)		das Problem (e)	problem
der Mord (e)	murder	die Umfrage (n)	survey
die Drogenszene	drug scene		
drogenabhängig	addicted to drugs	die Mauer (n)	wall
		das Jahrhundert (e)	century
die Gefahr (en)	danger	die Zukunft	future
gefährlich	dangerous		

66

◆ Higher words

die Wende	reunification
der Gastarbeiter (-)	immigrant
die Gastarbeiterin (nen)	worker
der Rassismus	racism
die Armut	poverty
der Aussiedler (-)	immigrant of
die Aussiedlerin (nen)	German origin
der Einwanderer (-)	immigrant
die Einwanderin (nen)	
der Flüchtling (e)	refugee
Zuflucht suchen	to seek refuge
bekämpfen	to fight against
das Vorurteil (e)	prejudice
arm	poor
obdachlos	homeless
der Obdachlose (n)	homeless
die Obdachlose (n)	person
sich anmelden	to register
die Gesellschaft (en)	society
die Demonstration (en)	demonstration
die Dritte Welt	Third World
die entwickelten Länder (pl)	developed countries

das Entwicklungsland (-länder)	developing country
der Einbrecher (-)	burglar
die Einbrecherin (nen)	
einbrechen	to break in
der Einbruch (¨e)	burglary
der Ladendiebstahl (-stähle)	shoplifting
die Gewalt	violence
der Schläger (-)	thug
schlagen	to hit
überfallen	to attack
der Rowdy (s)	hooligan
der Vandalismus	vandalism
töten	to kill
tödlich	deadly
der Tod (Todesfälle)	death
umbringen	to kill
feindlich	hostile
die Waffe (n)	weapon
Drogen probieren	to try drugs
der Drogensüchtige (n)	drug addict
die Drogensüchtige (n)	

THE WEATHER

◆ Foundation words

das Klima (s)	climate
das Wetter	weather
der Wetterbericht (e)	weather report
die Wettervorhersage (n)	weather forecast
der Grad (-)	degree
die Temperatur (en)	temperature
die Höchsttemperatur	peak temperature
die Tiefsttemperatur	lowest temperature

der Wind (e)	wind
windig	windy
das Gewitter (-)	storm
der Sturm (¨e)	storm
stürmisch	stormy
der Blitz (e)	lightning
es blitzt	there's lightning
der Donner	thunder
die Donnerschläge (pl)	thunder
es donnert	it's thundering

der Nebel (-)	fog	der Regen	rain
neblig	foggy	regnen	to rain
frieren	to freeze	regnerisch	rainy
der Frost (¨e)	frost	der Schauer (-)	shower
das Glatteis	ice on the road	feucht	damp
der Schnee	snow	nass	wet
schneien	to snow	schlechtes Wetter	bad weather
wechselhaft	changeable		
kalt	cold	die Sonne (n)	sun
kühl	cool	sonnig	sunny
die Wolke (n)	cloud	scheinen	to shine
wolkig	cloudy	trocken	dry
bedeckt	overcast	warm	warm
bewölkt	cloudy	herrlich	lovely
wolkenlos	cloudless	gutes Wetter	good weather

◆ **Foundation phrases**

Wie wird das Wetter morgen sein?	What will the weather be like tomorrow?
Es soll regnen.	It's supposed to rain.
Mir ist heiß/kalt.	I'm hot/cold.
Am Vormittag wird es schön sein.	It will be nice in the morning.
In der Nacht wird es schneien.	It will snow at night.
Im Winter ist es gewöhnlich kalt.	It's usually cold in winter.
Im Herbst ist es oft neblig.	It's often foggy in the autumn.
Bei so heißem Wetter kommt oft ein Gewitter.	Such hot weather often brings a storm.
In dieser Gegend regnet es viel.	It rains a lot in this area.
Es hat gestern stark geregnet.	It rained heavily yesterday.

◆ **Higher words**

voraussagen	to predict	der Niederschlag (¨e)	rain
aussehen	to appear	gießen	to pour (down)
der Dunst (¨e)	mist	der Hagel	hail
dunstig	misty	hageln	to hail
die Hitze	heat	aufklären	to brighten up
schwül	sultry, muggy	heiter	bright
mild	mild	die Aufheiterung (en)	brighter period
		der Hochdruck	high pressure

◆ **Higher phrases**

Es sieht nach Regen aus.	It looks like rain.
Hoffentlich bleibt es trocken.	I hope it'll stay dry.
wegen des schlechten Wetters	because of the bad weather
Es wurde äußerst kalt.	It got extremely cold.

What's the weather like today?

Deutscher Wetterdienst

Zeichenerklärung:

◯	wolkenlos
◖	heiter
◐	halb bedeckt
◕	wolkig
●	bedeckt
	Nordwind 10 km/h
	Ostwind 20 km/h
	Südwind 30 km/h
	Westwind 40 km/h
	Temperatur in Grad Celsius
≡	Nebel
𝟇	Sprühregen
●	Regen
⌢⌣	gefrierender Regen
✳	Schnee
▽	Schauer
◿	Gewitter
///	Niederschlagsgebiet
	Warmfront
	Okklusion
▲ ▲	Kaltfront am Boden
△ △	Kaltfront in der Höhe
⇒	Luftströmung warm
▬▶	Luftströmung kalt
H	Hochdruckzentrum
T	Tiefdruckzentrum
h	Sekundär Hoch
t	Sekundär Tief
⁓	Isobaren

THE NATURAL ENVIRONMENT

◆ Foundation words

die Erde	earth	die Welle (n)	wave
der Himmel (-)	sky	die Küste (n)	coast
der Stern (e)	star	das Meer (e)	sea
die Luft	air	die Insel (n)	island
die Natur	nature	der Rand (¨er)	edge
der Stein (e)	stone	das Feld (er)	field
das Gebirge (-)	mountain range	das Gras (¨er)	grass
der Berg (e)	mountain	die Pflanze (n)	plant
der Hügel (-)	hill	der Baum (Bäume)	tree
der Gipfel (-)	summit	der Tannenbaum	fir tree
das Tal (¨er)	valley	(-bäume)	
tief	low, deep	der Dschungel (-)	jungle
flach	flat	der Wald (¨er)	forest, wood
der Fluss (¨e)	river		

69

◆ **Foundation phrases**

Ich wohne am Rande eines Waldes.	I live on the edge of a wood.
Die Luft ist sehr rein hier.	The air is very pure here.
Das ist nicht weit von der Küste.	That's not far from the coast.

◆ **Higher words**

steil	steep	der Sonnenuntergang	sunset
der Bach ("e)	stream	(-gänge)	
die Hecke (n)	hedge	der Mond (e)	moon
der Teich (e)	pond	die Wiese (n)	meadow
das Ufer (-)	bank	die Felsen (pl)	cliffs
		schmal	narrow
die Ebbe (n)	low tide		
die Flut (en)	high tide	das Erdbeben (-)	earthquake
die Überschwemmung (en)	flood	zerstören	to destroy
fließen	to flow	der Einsturz ("e)	collapse
der Sonnenaufgang (-gänge)	sunrise	die Dürre (n)	drought

◆ **Higher phrases**

Es ist sehr flach im Vergleich zu Bayern.	It's very flat compared to Bavaria.
Die Landschaft hier ist nicht so hügelig.	The countryside here is not as hilly.

ENVIRONMENTAL ISSUES

◆ **Foundation words**

die Welt (en)	world	umweltfreundlich	good for the environment
die Umwelt	environment		
der Lärm	noise	umweltfeindlich	bad for the environment
das Geräusch (e)	sound		
der Müll	rubbish	der Umweltschutz	environmental protection
die Verschmutzung	pollution		

◆ **Higher words**

der saure Regen	acid rain	die Mülltonne (n)	dustbin
die Aussicht (en)	view, outlook	das Altpapier	waste paper to recycle
die Warnung (en)	warning		
der Delfin (e)	dolphin	die Pfandflasche (n)	returnable bottle
der Regenwald ("er)	rain forest		
verschwinden	to disappear	die Einwegflasche (n)	non-returnable bottle
die Ursache (n)	cause		
		recyceln	to recycle
der Abfall (-fälle)	litter	wieder verwerten	to use again
der Haushaltsmüll	household rubbish	wegwerfen	to throw away

verschwenden	to waste	verpesten	to pollute
die Verschwendung	waste	das Kernkraftwerk (e)	nuclear power station
die Wiederverwertung	recycling	der Strom	electricity
die Atmosphäre (n)	atmosphere	der Ölteppich (e)	oil slick
der Auspuff (e)	car exhaust	die Chemikalie (n)	chemical
die Abgase (pl)	exhaust fumes	das Pestizid (e)	pesticide
das Schwefeldioxid	sulphur dioxide	die Ozonschicht	ozone layer
der Rauch	smoke	der Treibhauseffekt	greenhouse effect
vergiften	to poison		

What are these stickers about?

HOW TO LEARN

VOCABULARY

Some people learn best by seeing words written down, others like to hear them. It might help you to record words and phrases on tape, so that you have to read them out, and then you can listen to them, perhaps on a walkman:

- Record a German word or phrase.
- Leave a short gap (three seconds).
- Record the English meaning.
- When you listen to the tape later, say the English word in the gap.
- Then listen to see if you were right.

HOW TO USE A DICTIONARY

A good dictionary will help you with proper names as well as other aspects of language. So you can look up "Bavaria" and find *Bayern*. Most names of towns remain the same, of course, so London is *London* and Madrid is *Madrid*. Your dictionary may even have a list of countries.

Use your dictionary to find the German for:

1 The Atlantic ....

2 California ....

3 A pound sterling ....

(Answer on page 98)

T I P P S ◆ T I P P S ◆ T I P P S ◆ T I P P S

Home Town

IN THE AREA

◆ Foundation words

das Dorf ("er)	village
die Stadt ("e)	town
die Hauptstadt ("e)	capital
die Großstadt ("e)	city
die Hafenstadt ("e)	harbour town
die Innenstadt ("e)	town centre
der Einwohner (-)	inhabitant
die Einwohnerin (nen)	
die Stadtmitte (n)	town centre
der Vorort (e)	suburb
die Landschaft (en)	scenery
die Gegend (en)	area, region
die Industrie (n)	industry
der Bauernhof (-höfe)	farm
die Brücke (n)	bridge
der Kanal (Kanäle)	canal
der Tiergarten (")	zoo
der Park (s)	park
der Ort (e)	place
das Gebäude (-)	building
der Dom (e)	cathedral
die Kirche (n)	church
die Kapelle (n)	chapel
das Schloss ("er)	castle
die Burg (en)	old castle
das Denkmal ("er)	monument
der Turm ("e)	tower
das Rathaus (-häuser)	town hall
die Sparkasse (n)	savings bank

die Bank (en)	bank
das Postamt (-ämter)	post office
die Wäscherei (en)	laundry
der Parkplatz (-plätze)	carpark
das Parkhaus (-häuser)	multi-storey carpark
die Polizeiwache (n)	police station
der Marktplatz (-plätze)	market place
der Markt ("e)	market
die Fußgängerzone (n)	pedestrian zone
der Laden (")	shop
das Geschäft (e)	shop
das Kaufhaus (-häuser)	department store
das Warenhaus (-häuser)	department store
das Einkaufszentrum (-zentren)	shopping centre
der Supermarkt (-märkte)	supermarket
die Bäckerei (en)	baker's
die Konditorei (en)	cake shop
die Metzgerei (en)	butcher's
das Schreibwarengeschäft (e)	stationer's
die Drogerie (n)	chemist's
die Apotheke (n)	(dispensing) chemist's
die Buchhandlung (en)	bookshop

◆ Foundation phrases

Es ist eine mittelgroße Stadt.	It's a medium-sized town.
Es ist nicht sehr groß, aber es ist schön.	It's not very big, but it's pretty.
Es gibt eine alte Kirche.	There's an old church.
Ich wohne auf dem Lande.	I live in the country.
Es gibt viel zu sehen.	There's lots to see.
Die Gegend ist herrlich.	The area is lovely.

HOME TOWN

◆ Higher words

die Partnerstadt (-städte)	twin town
der Stadtteil (e)	district, part of town
das Stadtviertel (-)	district, part of town
städtisch	urban
der Stadtbewohner (-)	town/city
die Stadtbewohnerin (nen)	dweller
der Stadtkreis (e)	borough
die Heimatstadt (-städte)	home town
das Gebiet (e)	area
das Wohngebiet (e)	residential area
der Bezirk (e)	district
die Umgebung (en)	surrounding area
der Brunnen (-)	fountain

die Festhalle (n)	festival hall
die Eissporthalle (n)	skating rink
das Revier (e)	police station
der Jachthafen (-häfen)	yacht marina
der Jahrmarkt (-märkte)	funfair
der Flohmarkt (-märkte)	second-hand market
die Grünanlage (n)	green space
das Eisenwarengeschäft (e)	hardware shop
der Weinberg (e)	vineyard
die Weinernte (n)	grape harvest
die Weinlese (n)	grape harvest
der Weinbauer (n)	vine grower
die Weinbäuerin (nen)	

◆ Higher phrases

Meine Heimatstadt liegt in einem Industriegebiet. — My home town is in an industrial area.

Es fehlt nur ein schöner Park. — All that's missing is a nice park.

FINDING THE WAY

◆ Foundation words

hinter	behind
bis	up to, until
durch	through
entlang	along
gegenüber	opposite
nach	after
über	over
unter	under
vor	in front of
zwischen	between
in der Nähe	nearby

dort drüben	over there
geradeaus	straight on
links	left
rechts	right
weit	far
abbiegen	to turn off
die Richtung (en)	direction
die Landkarte (n)	map
der Stadtplan (-pläne)	street plan
die Landstraße (n)	country road
der Wegweiser (-)	road sign

73

der Weg (e)	way	die Ecke (n)	corner
die Sperre (n)	barrier	die Kreuzung (en)	crossroads
die Allee (n)	avenue	die Hauptstraße (n)	main road
die Gasse (n)	alley	die Autobahn (en)	motorway

◆ Foundation phrases

Gibt es eine Apotheke hier in der Nähe?	Is there a chemist's near here?
Wo ist die nächste Tankstelle?	Where's the next petrol station?
Wie komme ich zum Schloss, bitte?	How do I get to the castle, please?
Es gibt einen Parkplatz am Markt.	There's a carpark in the market.
Sie gehen hier rechts/geradeaus.	You go right/straight on here.
Sie nehmen die erste Straße links.	You take the first street on the left.
Sie gehen bis zur Kirche.	You go as far as the church.
Gegenüber ist eine Bushaltestelle.	There's a bus stop opposite.
Ist es weit?	Is it far?
Das ist nur zwei Minuten von hier.	That's only two minutes from here.
Das ist hier in der Nähe.	It's nearby.
Am besten fahren Sie mit dem Bus.	It's best to take the bus.

◆ Higher words

folgen	to follow	der Pfad (e)	path, trail
die Nebenstraße (n)	side road	der Bürgersteig (e)	pavement
sich verfahren	to get lost (in car)	der Zebrastreifen (-)	pedestrian crossing
sich verlaufen	to get lost (on foot)	sich auskennen	to know one's way round
überqueren	to cross		
die Kurve (n)	bend in the road		

◆ Higher phrases

Wo kann ich mich erkundigen?	Where can I make enquiries?
Ich habe mich verlaufen.	I've got lost. (on foot)
Überqueren Sie die Brücke.	Cross the bridge.
Ich kenne mich hier gut aus.	I know this area very well.

HOW TO LEARN

VOCABULARY
Although you need to learn the genders of nouns, there are some endings that can help you.

Look back at nouns in this section, and write down the gender these endings show:

1 Kreuzung, Richtung   ....

2 Metzgerei, Konditorei   ....

3 Landschaft   ....

(Answer on page 98)

HOW TO USE A DICTIONARY
Where possible, stick to words you already know when speaking and writing. Using the dictionary a lot will take up too much time and could tempt you to try to say things you cannot do yet. Play safe!! Learning words in context rather than in isolation helps. Try to learn the phrases given in this book as well as the lists of vocabulary.

Shopping and Eating

SHOPPING

◆ Foundation words

die Geschäftszeit (en)	business hours
schließen	to close
geschlossen	closed, shut
öffnen	to open
offen	open
die Öffnungszeit (en)	opening time
das Untergeschoss (e)	lower floor
das Obergeschoss (e)	upper floor
das Stockwerk (e)	floor
die Etage (n)	floor
der Notausgang (-gänge)	emergency exit
der Eingang ("e)	entrance
ziehen	to pull
drücken	to push
die Rolltreppe (n)	escalator
das Angebot (e)	offer
das Sonderangebot (e)	special offer
verkaufen	to sell
der Ausverkauf	sale
der Schlussverkauf	sale
die Mehrwertsteuer	value added tax
MWSt.	VAT

das Schaufenster (-)	shop window
die Einkaufsliste (n)	shopping list
der Kunde (n) die Kundin (nen)	customer
die Schlange (n)	queue
Schlange stehen	to queue
die Tüte (n)	packet, carrier bag
billig	cheap
preiswert	cheap
kostbar	valuable
teuer	expensive
kostenlos	free
insgesamt	altogether
das Geld	money
bezahlen	to pay
der Geldbeutel (-)	purse
die Qualität	quality
sich beschweren	to complain
die Garantie (n)	guarantee
umtauschen	to change

See page 72 for places and shops in town.

◆ Foundation phrases

Wann macht die Bäckerei auf?	When does the baker's open?
Wann schließt die Post?	When does the post office close?
Sie ist bis vierzehn Uhr geschlossen.	It's closed until two o'clock.
Wann machen Sie zu?	When do you close?
Es ist samstagnachmittags geschlossen.	It's closed on Saturday afternoons.
Das ist mir zu teuer.	That's too expensive for me.
Das ist im zweiten Stock.	That's on the second floor.
einen Schaufensterbummel machen	to window shop

◆ Higher words

der Rabatt (e)	reduction	liefern	to deliver
erhältlich	available	der Lieferwagen (-)	delivery van
die Anzahlung (en)	deposit		
		einwickeln	to gift-wrap
der Ladenbesitzer (-)	shopkeeper	die Bezahlung (en)	payment
die Ladenbesitzerin		die Quittung (en)	receipt
(nen)		der Kassenzettel (-)	till receipt
außer Betrieb	out of order	die Theke (n)	counter
die Betriebsferien (pl)	annual holiday	einschließlich	including
der Feierabend (e)	closing time	wertvoll	valuable
der Feiertag (e)	holiday	wertlos	worthless
der Ruhetag (e)	day off		

◆ Higher phrases

Ich möchte mein Geld zurück(bekommen).	I'd like to get my money back.
Ich habe die Quittung nicht behalten.	I haven't kept the receipt.
Sehen Sie sich unverbindlich um.	You are welcome to browse.
In einem Supermarkt findet man alles unter einem Dach.	In a supermarket you can find everything under one roof.

CLOTHES AND SOUVENIRS

◆ Foundation words

alles	everything	die Baumwolle	cotton
die Farbe (n)	colour	die Wolle	wool
schick	smart		
die Mode (n)	fashion	das Kostüm (e)	suit (female)
modisch	fashionable	der Anzug (-züge)	suit
altmodisch	old-fashioned	der Jogginganzug	tracksuit
		der Trainingsanzug	tracksuit
die Größe (n)	size	der Schlafanzug	pyjamas
anprobieren	to try on	der Badeanzug	swimming
passen	to fit		costume
tragen	to wear		
		das Hemd (en)	shirt
die Kleidung	clothes	die Bluse (n)	blouse
der Stoff (e)	material	das T-Shirt (s)	T-shirt
das Leder	leather	das Kleid (er)	dress

der Rock (¨e)	skirt		das Geschenk (e)	present
die Jeans (-)	pair of jeans		das Souvenir (s)	souvenir
die Hose (n)	pair of trousers		das Andenken (-)	souvenir
der Pulli (s)	pullover			
der Pullover (-)	pullover		das Parfüm (e)	perfume
die Jacke (n)	jacket		das Armband (-bänder)	bracelet
der Mantel (¨)	coat		der Schmuck	jewellery
			der Ohrring (e)	earring
die Badehose (n)	trunks		der Ring (e)	ring
die Unterhose (n)	underpants		die Uhr (en)	watch, clock
die Unterwäsche	underwear		die Armbanduhr (en)	watch
der Hut (¨e)	hat		der Gürtel (-)	belt
die Mütze (n)	cap		das Taschentuch	handkerchief
der Schal (s)	scarf		(-tücher)	
der Handschuh (e)	glove		die Handtasche (n)	handbag
die Krawatte (n)	tie		die Brieftasche (n)	wallet
der Schlips (e)	tie		das Portemonnaie (s)	purse
			der Regenschirm (e)	umbrella
die Socke (n)	sock		das Feuerzeug (e)	lighter
die Strumpfhose (n)	tights		der Aschenbecher (-)	ash tray
der Schuh (e)	shoe		die Sonnenbrille (n)	sunglasses
die Sandale (n)	sandal		die Sache (n)	thing
der Stiefel (-)	boot		das Plakat (e)	poster

◆ Foundation phrases

Ich möchte einen Pulli aus Wolle.	I'd like a woollen pullover.
Welche Größe?	What size?
Haben Sie diese Krawatte in Blau?	Have you got this tie in blue?
Wie gefällt dir meine Jacke?	How do you like my jacket?
Diese Schuhe sind zu teuer.	These shoes are too expensive.
Ich nehme diesen Ring.	I'll take this ring.
Diese Jacke ist mir zu klein/groß.	This jacket is too small/big for me.
Haben Sie etwas Kleineres/Billigeres?	Have you got anything smaller/cheaper?
Kann ich das anprobieren?	Can I try that on?

Wenn du etwas kaufst, was ist für dich wichtig?

Wichtig für mich ist,

	gesamt %	männlich %	weiblich %
... dass es modisch ist und dem neuesten Trend entspricht	11,4	10,7	11,7
... dass es meinem persönlichen Stil entspricht	75,2	69,4	80,7
... dass es eine teure Marke ist, die auffällt	3,0	3,2	2,8
... dass ich überlegt kaufe, Preise und Qualität vergleiche	45,5	46,2	45,3
... nichts zu kaufen, was gesundheits- oder umweltschädlich ist	32,1	29,8	34,6
... keine Produkte aus politisch umstrittenen Ländern zu kaufen	11,3	10,1	12,6

◆ **Higher words**

reinigen	to clean	der Büstenhalter (-)	bra
die Reinigung (en)	dry cleaner's		
der Waschsalon (s)	launderette	die Puppe (n)	doll
die Klamotten (pl)	clothes	das Kuscheltier (e)	cuddly toy
die Marke (n)	brand, make		
die Konfektion (en)	clothing	gestreift	striped
der Reißverschluss (¨e)	zip	kariert	checked
die Halskette (n)	necklace	gemustert	patterned
die Seide	silk	eingelaufen	shrunk
der Regenmantel (¨)	raincoat	in... gekleidet	dressed in
der Sakko (s)	jacket		

◆ **Higher phrases**

Ich schaue nur.	I'm just looking.
Haben Sie das eine Nummer größer?	Have you got that one size bigger?
Es passt nicht zu meinem Kleid.	It doesn't go with my dress.
Ich möchte diese Jacke reinigen lassen.	I'd like to have this jacket dry-cleaned.

What can you buy at this department store?

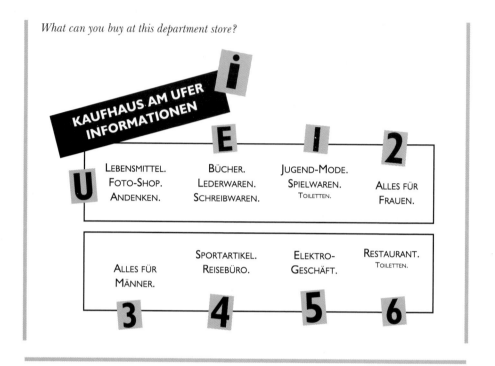

FOOD AND DRINK

◆ **Foundation words**

schmecken	to taste	die Zutaten (pl)	ingredients
der Geschmack (¨e)	taste	das Rezept (e)	recipe
lecker	tasty, delicious	die Lebensmittel (pl)	food
frisch	fresh	das Päckchen (-)	small packet
scharf	spicy	das Paket (e)	packet
süß	sweet	die Schachtel (n)	box
sauer	sour, bitter	die Flasche (n)	bottle
		die Dose (n)	tin
kochen	to cook	die Scheibe (n)	slice
braten	to fry, roast	das Stück (e)	piece
grillen	to grill, barbecue	die Hälfte (n)	half
		das Gemüse (-)	vegetable(s)
die Pfanne (n)	pan	die Karotte (n)	carrot
das Picknick (s)	picnic	die Erbse (n)	pea
die Mahlzeit (en)	meal	die Zwiebel (n)	onion

80

der Kopfsalat (e)	lettuce	die Sahne	cream
das Sauerkraut	pickled cabbage	die Schlagsahne	whipped cream
der Kohl (köpfe)	cabbage	das Omelett (s)	omelette
der Rotkohl (köpfe)	red cabbage	das Ei (er)	egg
die Bohne (n)	bean	das Rührei	scrambled egg
die Gurke (n)	cucumber	das Spiegelei	fried egg
die Kartoffel (n)	potato	der Käse (sorten)	cheese
die Salzkartoffel (n)	boiled potato	die Milch	milk
die Bratkartoffel (n)	fried potato		
die Pommes (pl)	chips	das Fleisch	meat
die Pommes frites (pl)	chips	der Fisch (e)	fish
der Pilz (e)	mushroom	die Frikadelle (n)	rissole, meatball
der Champignon (s)	mushroom	das Kalbfleisch	veal
der Blumenkohl	cauliflower	das Kotelett (s)	chop, cutlet
		das Schnitzel (-)	schnitzel, cutlet
		das Schweinefleisch	pork
das Obst (sorten)	fruit	das Würstchen (-)	small sausage
die Frucht (¨e)	fruit	die Wurst (¨e)	sausage
die Ananas (-)	pineapple	die Bockwurst	(type of)
das Kompott (e)	stewed fruit		sausage
die Zitrone (n)	lemon	die Bratwurst	fried sausage
die Traube (n)	grape	die Currywurst	sausage in curry
die Tomate (n)	tomato		sauce
die Erdbeere (n)	strawberry	die Leberwurst	liver sausage
die Himbeere (n)	raspberry	der Aufschnitt	sliced cold
die Aprikose (n)	apricot		meats
die Pflaume (n)	plum	der Schinken (-)	ham
die Birne (n)	pear	das Hähnchen (-)	chicken
die Apfelsine (n)	orange	der Speck	bacon
die Orange (n)	orange	das Rindfleisch	beef
der Pfirsich (e)	peach	der Eintopf (¨e)	stew
die Banane (n)	banana		
der Apfel (¨)	apple	die Soße (n)	sauce, gravy
die Kirsche (n)	cherry	der Pfeffer	pepper
		das Salz	salt
das Brot (e)	bread	der Senf (e)	mustard
das Brötchen (-)	bread roll	der Essig	vinegar
die Butter	butter	der Reis	rice
das Butterbrot (e)	buttered bread	die Suppe (n)	soup
die Margarine	margarine		
die Marmelade (n)	jam	die Süßigkeiten (pl)	sweets
das Mehl	flour	die Chips (pl)	crisps

die Praline (n)	chocolate	der Fruchtsaft	fruit juice
die Schokolade (n)	chocolate	der Apfelsaft	apple juice
das Bonbon (s)	sweet	der Orangensaft	orange juice
der Kakao (s)	cocoa	die Cola (s)	cola
das Gebäck	biscuits, pastries	die Limo (s)	lemonade
das Eis	ice cream	die Limonade (n)	lemonade
der/das Joghurt (s)	yogurt	das Wasser (-)	water
der Kuchen (-)	cake	das Mineralwasser (-)	mineral water
die Torte (n)	tart, gateau	der Sprudel (-)	mineral water
der Honig	honey		
der Keks (e)	biscuit	die Schüssel (n)	bowl
der Kaugummi (s)	chewing gum	die Untertasse (n)	saucer
der Zucker	sugar	der Becher (-)	mug
die Nuss ("e)	nut	das Kännchen (-)	pot
		die Kaffeekanne (n)	coffee pot
das Getränk (e)	drink	der Teller (-)	plate
trinken	to drink	die Teekanne (n)	teapot
das Bier (e)	beer	die Tasse (n)	cup
der Sekt (sorten)	sparkling wine	die Gabel (n)	fork
der Wein (e)	wine	das Glas ("er)	glass
der Tee (s)	tea	der Löffel (-)	spoon
der Kaffee (s)	coffee	das Messer (-)	knife
der Saft ("e)	juice		

◆ Foundation phrases

Ist das alles?	Is that all?
Sonst noch etwas?	Anything else?
Was kostet das?	How much is that?
Das wär's, danke.	That's all, thank you.
Fünfhundert Gramm Wurst, bitte.	Five hundred grammes of sausage, please.
Zwei Liter Milch, bitte.	Two litres of milk, please.
Ich möchte ein Stück Käse, bitte.	I'd like a piece of cheese, please.
Haben Sie eine Flasche Cola?	Have you got a bottle of cola?
Wir haben keine Apfelsinen mehr.	We haven't got any oranges left.
Wo kann ich Obst kaufen?	Where can I buy some fruit?
Haben Sie noch einige Pfirsiche?	Have you got any peaches left?
Ein Pfund Tomaten, bitte.	Half a kilo of tomatoes, please.
Ein Kilo Orangen, bitte.	A kilo of oranges, please.
Ich möchte auch eine Packung Chips.	I'd also like a packet of crisps.
Eine kleine Schachtel Pralinen, bitte.	A small box of chocolates, please.

Es schmeckt sehr gut.	It tastes very good.
Das ist mir zu scharf.	It's too spicy for me.
Ich esse sehr gern Wurst.	I love sausage.
Ich trinke gern Orangensaft.	I like orange juice.
Ich esse nicht gern Currywurst.	I don't like sausage in curry sauce.
Wir essen oft Pommes frites.	We often eat chips.
Wir trinken gewöhnlich Kaffee.	We usually drink coffee.

Möchtest du ein bisschen Käse?	Would you like a little cheese?
Ich habe keinen Löffel.	I haven't got a spoon.
Gib mir das Salz, bitte.	Pass me the salt, please.
Könnten Sie mir bitte das Brot geben?	Could you pass me the bread, please?
Ich möchte noch etwas Zucker, bitte.	I'd like a little more sugar, please.
Leider haben wir kein Brot.	Unfortunately we've got no bread.

◆ Higher words

riechen	to smell	die Forelle (n)	trout
köstlich	delicious	die Meeresfrüchte (pl)	sea food
das Besteck (e)	cutlery	ein belegtes Brot	an open
das Geschirr	crockery	(belegte Brote)	sandwich
die Zutaten (pl)	ingredients	der Lebkuchen (-)	gingerbread
schälen	to peel	der Sauerbraten (-)	braised
würzen	to season		beef
das Kraut (¨er)	herb	der Schweinebraten (-)	roast pork
fett	fatty	die Blätterteigpastete (n)	*vol-au-vent*
mager	low-fat	der Stollen (-)	German
ungesund	unhealthy		Christmas cake
der Geruch (¨e)	smell		

◆ Higher phrases

Das riecht köstlich.	That smells delicious.
Das bekommt mir nicht.	That doesn't agree with me.
Mindestens haltbar bis…	Can be kept until at least…

Sage mir wie du frühstückst...

Frage 1: Wann stehst du gewöhnlich morgens auf?

a) Morgens? Morgens gehe ich ins Bett! ○

b) Um 6 Uhr. ○

c) Wenn ich wach werde. ○

d) Zwischen 9 und 11 Uhr. ○

Frage 2: Warum?

a) Weil der Hahn kräht. ○

b) Weil mein Chef anruft. ○

c) Weil ich Durst habe. ○

d) Weil mein Butler klopft. ○

Frage 3: Was machst du dann?

a) Ich renne zur Bushaltestelle. ○

b) Ich mache erstmal eine Dose Bier auf. ○

c) Ich mache Frühstück. ○

d) Ich gehe immer frühstücken. ○

Frage 4: Was gibt's zu essen?

a) Nichts. ○

b) Hab' ich doch schon gesagt, eine Dose Bier. ○

c) Meerrettich, Lachs, Sekt, Roter Kaviar... ○

d) Noch mal Toast, Ei, Kaffee, Brei. ○

Frage 5: Was liest du beim Frühstück?

a) Die *Rheinische Post*. ○

b) Den *Express*. ○

c) Das Etikett der Bierdose. ○

d) Die *Zeit*. ○

Frage 6: Worüber redest du?

a) Politik, Religion, Wirtschaft. ○

b) Reden? Mit wem? ○

c) Das Wetter, über Leute, die nicht da sind... ○

d) Theater, Kunst, Mode, Philosophie... ○

Frage 7: Wie viel gibst du täglich für dein Frühstück aus?

a) 5,50 Euro ○

b) Zwischen 1 und 20 Euro. ○

c) Weiß nicht, zahle mit American Express. ○

d) 0,59 Euro. ○

Frage 8: Was machst du nach dem Frühstück?

a) Ich gehe zur Arbeit. ○

b) Ich gehe zum Frühschoppen in die Kneipe. ○

c) Dito, mit Zeitung. ○

d) Ich gehe ins Bett. ○

Now turn to page 99...

RESTAURANTS AND CAFÉS

◆ Foundation words

das Café (s)	café	der Nachtisch (e)	dessert
die Wurstbude (n)	sausage stand	die Nachspeise (n)	dessert
der Schnellimbiss (e)	snack bar	der Eisbecher (-)	sundae
die Imbissstube (n)	snack bar	die Erfrischung (en)	refreshment
die Selbstbedienung	self-service	zum Mitnehmen	take-away
die Kneipe (n)	pub	betrunken	drunk
das Wirtshaus (-häuser)	pub	hungrig	hungry
das Lokal (e)	pub	durstig	thirsty
die Gaststätte (n)	inn	gemütlich	cosy
das Gasthaus (-häuser)	inn	zahlen	to pay
der Gasthof (-höfe)	inn	die Quittung (en)	receipt
die Trinkhalle (n)	drinks kiosk	das Trinkgeld (er)	tip
		zusammen	together
die Preistafel (n)	price board		
die Tageskarte (n)	day's menu	kauen	to chew
die Speisekarte (n)	menu	satt	full up
das Menü (s)	set menu	guten Appetit	enjoy your meal
die Weinliste (n)	wine list	Prost	cheers
der Kellner (-)	waiter	zum Wohl	cheers
die Kellnerin (nen)	waitress	bedienen	to serve
bestellen	to order	behilflich	helpful
die Vorspeise (n)	starter	zugreifen	to help oneself
das Hauptgericht (e)	main course		

◆ Foundation phrases

Herr Ober!	Waiter!
Fräulein!	Waitress!
Haben Sie einen Tisch für drei Personen?	Have you got a table for three?
Die Speisekarte, bitte.	The menu, please.
Einmal Suppe.	One soup.
Zweimal Hähnchen mit Pommes frites.	Two chicken and chips.
Ich möchte ein Glas Cola.	I'd like a glass of cola.
Als Nachtisch hätte ich gern ein Eis.	For dessert, I'd like an ice cream.
Was für Eis haben Sie?	What sorts of ice cream have you got?
Gibt es noch etwas Suppe?	Is there any more soup?
Das Menü zu achtzehn Euro, bitte.	The eighteen-euro menu, please.
Was genau ist Schnitzel?	What is schnitzel exactly?
Der Kuchen war besonders gut.	The cake was particularly good.
Die Pommes frites waren kalt.	The chips were cold.
Zahlen, bitte.	The bill, please.
Was macht das, bitte?	What does that come to, please?

Which category do you come under?

Wer trinkt seinen Kaffee wie?

Über Geschmack lässt sich bekanntlich nicht streiten. Erst recht nicht, wenn es um die Art und Weise geht, wie jeder seinen Kaffee genießt. Traditionell bevorzugen 43 Prozent der Bundesbürger, wie unser Schaubild zeigt, ihren Kaffee mit Milch oder Kaffeesahne. Auch mit Milch und Zucker erfreut sich das Getränk großer Beliebtheit. Nur wenige trinken ihren Kaffee schwarz oder nur mit Zucker.

mit Milch oder Kaffeesahne
43%

mit Milch oder Kaffeesahne und Zucker
41%

nur mit Zucker
6%

schwarz
10%

◆ Higher words

probieren	to try	vegetarisch	vegetarian
die Spezialität (en)	speciality	empfehlen	to recommend
der Gang (¨e)	course	die Eisdiele (n)	ice-cream parlour
die Bedienung	service		
die Grillstube (n)	grill room	inbegriffen	included

◆ Higher phrases

Ist die Bedienung inbegriffen?	Is service included?
Was für belegte Brote haben Sie?	What sorts of sandwiches have you got?
Ich hätte lieber einen Tisch in der Ecke.	I'd rather have a table in the corner.
Die Rechnung stimmt nicht.	The bill isn't right.
Sie haben mir zu viel berechnet.	You've overcharged me.
Was können Sie mir empfehlen?	What can you recommend?

HOW TO LEARN

VOCABULARY

There are some words which look similar in German and English but which have quite different meanings. These are called "false friends", and you need to make a careful note of such words when you meet them.

See if you can get these words right without looking back:

1 *Chips* doesn't mean "chips", but ....

2 *Ein Rock* doesn't mean "a rock", but ....

3 *Ein Keks* doesn't mean "a cake", but ....

4 *Eine Dose* doesn't mean "a dose", but ....

(Answer on page 98)

HOW TO USE A DICTIONARY

If you are stuck when doing coursework, use your dictionary to come up with something in German. Always double-check to make sure you have found the right word: look up the German word in the German–English section to find its meaning, and possibly examples of its use.

◆ **Signs**

Fill in the missing part of these half-printed signs.

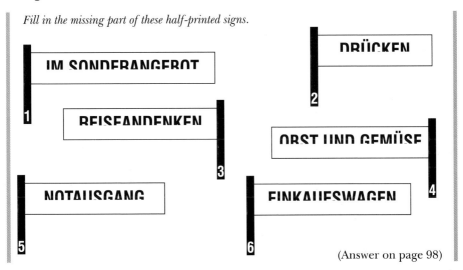

IM SONDERANGEBOT

1

REISEANDENKEN

3

NOTAUSGANG

5

DRÜCKEN

2

OBST UND GEMÜSE

EINKAUFSWAGEN

4

6

(Answer on page 98)

87

Transport

GENERAL

◆ Foundation words

fahren	to travel	dauern	to last
abfahren	to leave, set off	der Fahrschein (e)	ticket
die Abreise (n)	departure	die Fahrkarte (n)	ticket
die Abfahrt (en)	departure	der Wartesaal (-säle)	waiting room
ankommen	to arrive	die Auskunft (-künfte)	information
die Ankunft (-künfte)	arrival	der Fahrgast (-gäste)	passenger
pünktlich	on time	das Fahrgeld (er)	travel money
aussteigen	to get out	der Fahrplan (-pläne)	timetable
einsteigen	to get in	der Fahrpreis (e)	cost of travel
abholen	to meet, collect	Achtung!	attention!

◆ Foundation phrases

Wo kann ich Fahrkarten kaufen?	Where can I buy tickets?
Wann kommt er an?	When does it arrive?
Zurückbleiben, bitte!	Mind the doors!
Ihre Fahrkarten, bitte.	Your tickets, please.
Ich kann meine Fahrkarte nicht finden.	I can't find my ticket.
Wo ist die Auskunft?	Where is the information office?
Wann möchten Sie fahren?	When do you want to travel?
Wie lange dauert die Reise?	How long does the journey last?

◆ Higher words

die öffentlichen Verkehrsmittel	public transport	der Fahrkarten- automat (en)	ticket machine
das Schließfach ("er)	locker	das Verkehrsnetz (e)	transport network
die Gepäckaufbewahrung	left luggage office	das Fundbüro (s)	lost property office

Where would you see these signs?

ZU DEN GLEISEN

U3 Hauptbahnhof
U4 Flughafen
U5 Stadtmitte

H Bahnbus Europabus

✕ RESTAURANT
ℹ AUSKUNFT
☎ TELEFONE
🛏 WARTESAAL

TRAINS AND BUSES

◆ Foundation words

die Bahn (en)	railway	die Notbremse (n)	emergency brake
der Bahnhof (-höfe)	station		
der Hauptbahnhof	main station		
das Gleis (e)	platform	die Haltestelle (n)	(bus) stop
der Bahnsteig (e)	platform	die Linie (n)	number (bus)
der Zug (¨e)	train	der Reisebus (se)	coach
der D-Zug (¨e)	fast non-stop train	der Einstieg (e)	entrance
		umsteigen	to change
der Eilzug (¨e)	fast stopping train	der Entwerter (-)	ticket-punching machine
der Intercity-Zug (¨e)	inter-city train	der Fahrkartenschalter (-)	ticket office
der Nahverkehrszug (¨e)	local train	zweiter Klasse	second class
der Personenzug (¨e)	passenger train	einfach	single
die S-Bahn (en)	suburban railway	hin und zurück	return
		die Rückfahrkarte (n)	return ticket
die U-Bahn (en)	underground	der Zuschlag (-schläge)	extra fare, supplement
die Straßenbahn (en)	tram		
das Abteil (e)	compartment	gültig	valid
der Nichtraucher (-)	non-smoker	kontrollieren	to check
die Nichtraucherin (nen)			

◆ Foundation phrases

Eine Rückfahrkarte nach Frankfurt, bitte.	A return ticket to Frankfurt, please.
Wann fährt der nächste Zug nach Bonn?	When does the next train go to Bonn?
Von welchem Gleis fährt der Zug ab?	Which platform does the train leave from?
Ist jemand zugestiegen?	Tickets, please. (Has anybody got on?)
Muss ich umsteigen?	Do I have to change?
Kann man mit der U-Bahn fahren?	Can you go by underground?
Fährt diese Straßenbahn zum Bahnhof?	Does this tram go to the station?
Welche Linie fährt in die Stadtmitte?	Which number goes to the town centre?
Fährt ein Bus dahin?	Is there a bus to there?
Es ist schneller mit dem Bus.	It's quicker by bus.

◆ **Higher words**

die Verbindung (en)	connection	die Schiene (n)	track
planmäßig	scheduled	entwerten	to punch
die Verspätung (en)	delay		(ticket)
verpassen	to miss	die Geldstrafe (n)	fine
annullieren	to cancel	die Rückfahrt (en)	return
der Bahnübergang	level crossing		journey
(-gänge)		die Fahrtdauer	time the
der Gepäckträger (-)	porter		journey takes
die Gepäckträgerin (nen)			

◆ **Higher phrases**

Der Zug hat eine Stunde Verspätung.   The train is running one hour late.

BOATS AND PLANES

◆ **Foundation words**

der Anschluss (-schlüsse)	connection	abfliegen	to take off
der Flug (¨e)	flight	der Abflug (-flüge)	take off
der Flughafen (-häfen)	airport		
das Flugzeug (e)	plane	die Fähre (n)	ferry
der Fluggast (-gäste)	(plane)	das Schiff (e)	boat, ship
	passenger	das Boot (e)	boat
landen	to land	an Bord	on board
fliegen	to fly	seekrank	seasick

◆ **Foundation phrases**

Wir sind an Bord gegangen.   We went on board.

◆ **Higher words**

der Rückflug (¨e)	return flight	die Landung (en)	landing (plane)
die Abflugszeit (en)	departure time	der Dampfer (-)	steamer
die Gepäckannahme	check-in	das Motorboot (e)	motorboat
die Gepäckausgabe	baggage reclaim	das Ruderboot (e)	rowing boat
aufhalten	to delay	die Überfahrt (en)	(boat) crossing

◆ **Higher phrases**

Haben Sie etwas zu verzollen?   Have you anything to declare?

PRIVATE TRANSPORT

◆ **Foundation words**

der Wagen (-)	car	die Selbstbedienung	self-service
das Auto (s)	car	das Benzin	petrol
der Lastwagen (-)	lorry	das Normalbenzin	regular petrol
das Motorrad (-räder)	motorbike	bleifrei	lead free
das Fahrrad (-räder)	bicycle	unverbleit	unleaded
das Mofa (s)	moped	das Superbenzin	four-star petrol
zu Fuß	on foot	das Öl (e)	oil
der Fußgänger (-)	pedestrian	der Reifen (-)	tyre
die Fußgängerin (nen)		der Luftdruck	air pressure

abschleppen	to tow away	fahren	to drive
die Werkstatt ("en)	garage (for repairs)	der Verkehr	traffic
		der Autofahrer (-)	driver
die Panne (n)	breakdown	die Autofahrerin (nen)	
funktionieren	to work	der Fahrgast (-gäste)	passenger
reparieren	to repair	der Führerschein (e)	driving licence
der Notruf (e)	emergency call	die Durchfahrt (en)	through road, thoroughfare
die Ampel (n)	traffic lights	die Vorfahrt	priority
die Verkehrsampel (n)	traffic lights	überholen	to overtake
das Schild (er)	sign	beschreiben	to describe
die Umleitung (en)	diversion	anhalten	to stop
die Ausfahrt (en)	exit		
die Einbahnstraße (n)	one-way street	die Bremse (n)	brake
die Bundesstraße (n)	A-road	bremsen	to brake
die Hauptverkehrszeit	rush hour	losfahren	to start driving
der Stau (s)	traffic jam	mitfahren	to accompany
die Autobahn (en)	motorway	mitkommen	to come along
der Rasthof (-höfe)	motorway services	einordnen	to get in lane
		die Meile (n)	mile
die Raststätte (n)	motorway services	der Kilometer (-)	kilometre
		freihalten	to keep free
die Baustelle (n)	roadworks	die Parkuhr (en)	parking meter
		das Parkverbot (e)	parking ban
die Tankstelle (n)	petrol station	parken	to park
die Autowäsche	car wash	der Kofferraum (-räume)	boot
tanken	to fill up with petrol	mieten	to hire

◆ Higher words

der Unfall (-fälle)	accident	das Steuerrad (-räder)	steering wheel
der Zusammenstoß (-stöße)	collision	der Scheinwerfer (-)	headlight
überfahren	to run over	der Sitz (e)	seat
Gas geben	to accelerate	die Windschutzscheibe (n)	windscreen
abschleppen	to tow away	die Gepäckablage (n)	luggage rack
die Ringstraße (n)	ringroad	der Rückspiegel (-)	rear-view mirror
das Autobahnnetz (e)	motorway network	rückwärts fahren	to reverse
die Autobahn- einmündung (en)	motorway junction	sich anschnallen	to fasten one's seatbelt
das Autobahnkreuz (e)	motorway intersection	der Sicherheitsgurt (e)	seatbelt
die Fahrbahn (en)	lane (of motorway)	die Stoßzeit (en)	rush hour
die Spur (en)	lane (of motorway)	das Fahrzeug (e)	vehicle
		das Zweirad (¨er)	two-wheeled vehicle
die Maut (en)	toll	die Geschwindigkeit (en)	speed
die Mautstelle (n)	toll booth	die Höchstgeschwindig- keit (en)	speed limit
der Rastplatz (-plätze)	layby	die Geschwindigkeits- kontrolle (n)	speed check
die Bauarbeiten (pl)	roadworks		
gesperrt	blocked	der Streifenwagen (-)	police car
der Kreisverkehr (sing.)	roundabout	der Zeuge (n) die Zeugin (nen)	witness
die Kurve (n)	bend	der Parkschein (e)	carpark ticket
vorsichtig	carefully	die Fahrschule (n)	driving school
		autofrei	car-free
beschädigen	to damage		
der Schaden (¨)	damage		
das Ersatzteil (e)	spare part		
der Abschleppdienst (e)	breakdown service		

◆ Higher phrases

Mein Auto muss zur Inspektion.   I need to get the car serviced.

Ich habe eine Reifenpanne.   I've got a flat tyre.

Einfahrt verboten   no entry

Abstand halten   to keep one's distance

Ich habe einen Schaden am Wagen.   My car's been damaged.

Er ist mit dem Auto verunglückt.   He's had a car accident.

What do these signs mean?

HOW TO LEARN

VOCABULARY
Some people try word association and other tricks to help them remember words. See if it works for you, and make up some of your own like these.

In a traffic jam, you just have to *Stau* (stay) put.

A lorry is so slow it is always the *Lastwagen* (last waggon) to arrive.

Always leave *Ampel* (ample) space to stop at a red traffic light.

HOW TO USE A DICTIONARY
Use the little words in brackets in your dictionary to help you find the right word. If you want to say "The cases are in the boot," and you look up the word "boot", you might find something like (AUT) next to the word *Kofferraum* to show you that this is a word you want when talking about automobiles.

T I P P S ◆ T I P P S

93

General

◆ Question words

wie	how
wann	when
wer	who
warum	why
was	what
wie viel	how much
wie viele	how many
welche	which
wo	where
woher	where from
wohin	where to

◆ Days

Montag	Monday
Dienstag	Tuesday
Mittwoch	Wednesday
Donnerstag	Thursday
Freitag	Friday
Samstag	Saturday
Sonntag	Sunday
der Wochentag (e)	weekday
das Wochenende (n)	weekend

◆ Months

Januar	January
Februar	February
März	March
April	April
Mai	May
Juni	June
Juli	July
August	August
September	September
Oktober	October
November	November
Dezember	December

◆ Seasons

der Frühling (e)	spring
der Sommer (-)	summer
der Herbst (e)	autumn
der Winter (-)	winter
im Frühling	in spring

◆ Colours

blau	blue
blond	blond
braun	brown
gelb	yellow
grau	grey
grün	green
lila	purple
orange	orange
rosa	pink
rot	red
schwarz	black
weiß	white
bunt	colourful
dunkel	dark
hell	light
kastanienbraun	chestnut

◆ Weights and measures

all	all
ein bisschen	a bit
einige	some
einzeln	single
etwas	a little
genug	enough
das Gramm (-)	gramme
das Kilo (-)	kilo
das Pfund (-)	pound, half kilo
der/das Liter (-)	litre
nichts	nothing
ein paar	a few
pro	per
viel	a lot
wenig	a little

◆ Numbers 0–19

null	nought
eins	one
zwei	two
drei	three
vier	four
fünf	five
sechs	six

sieben	seven
acht	eight
neun	nine
zehn	ten
elf	eleven
zwölf	twelve
dreizehn	thirteen
vierzehn	fourteen
fünfzehn	fifteen
sechzehn	sixteen
siebzehn	seventeen
achtzehn	eighteen
neunzehn	nineteen
anderthalb	one-and-a-half

◆ Numbers 20–1,000

zwanzig	twenty
dreißig	thirty
vierzig	forty
fünfzig	fifty
sechzig	sixty
siebzig	seventy
achtzig	eighty
neunzig	ninety
hundert	(one) hundred
zweihundert	two hundred
dreihundert	three hundred
vierhundert	four hundred
fünfhundert	five hundred
sechshundert	six hundred
siebenhundert	seven hundred
achthundert	eight hundred
neunhundert	nine hundred
tausend	(one) thousand

◆ Numbers 1st–30th

erste	first
zweite	second
dritte	third
vierte	fourth
fünfte	fifth
sechste	sixth
siebte	seventh
achte	eighth
neunte	ninth
zehnte	tenth
elfte	eleventh
zwölfte	twelfth
dreizehnte	thirteenth
achtzehnte	eighteenth
neunzehnte	nineteenth
zwanzigste	twentieth
dreißigste	thirtieth

◆ Clock time

Wie viel Uhr ist es?	What's the time?
Es ist…	It's…
zwei Uhr	two o'clock
fünf nach zwei	five past two
zehn nach zwei	ten past two
Viertel nach zwei	a quarter past two
zwanzig nach zwei	twenty past two
fünf vor halb drei	twenty-five past two
halb drei	half past two
fünf nach halb drei	twenty-five to three
zwanzig vor drei	twenty to three
Viertel vor drei	a quarter to three
zehn vor drei	ten to three
fünf vor drei	five to three
Um sechs Uhr.	At six o'clock.

◆ Time expressions

der Morgen (-)	morning
der Nachmittag (e)	afternoon
der Abend (e)	evening
die Nacht ("e)	night
jeden Tag	every day
täglich	daily
wöchentlich	weekly
heutzutage	nowadays
am nächsten Tag	on the next day
bald	soon
sofort	at once
gestern	yesterday

95

vorgestern	the day before yesterday	**♦ Adjectives**	
vor kurzem	a short while ago	allein	alone
		eigen	own
		einzig	single
neulich	recently	zahlreich	numerous
heute	today	früh	early
morgen	tomorrow	genau	exact
übermorgen	the day after tomorrow	gleich	same
		kaputt	broken
jetzt	now	klar	clear
dann	then	leer	empty
nachher	afterwards	voll	full
später	later	nötig	necessary
im Voraus	in advance	nützlich	useful
		rund	round
zuerst	first of all	schmutzig	dirty
endlich	at last	toll	great
immer	always	typisch	typical
nie	never	falsch	wrong
manchmal	sometimes	wahr	true
selten	rarely	wichtig	important
oft	often		
schon	already		
noch nicht	not yet		
plötzlich	suddenly	**♦ Verbs**	
von Zeit zu Zeit	occasionally	beschließen	to decide
gewöhnlich	usually	brauchen	to need
		denken	to think
♦ Prepositions		erreichen	to reach
auf	on	folgen	to follow
aus	out of	gefallen	to please
außer	except	gehören	to belong to
bei	at the house of	geschehen	to happen
für	for	hoffen	to hope
gegen	against	bringen	to bring
mit	with	holen	to fetch
nach	after	nehmen	to take
neben	next to	lachen	to laugh
ohne	without	sich setzen	to sit down
seit	since	sitzen	to be sitting
um	around	verlieren	to lose
von	from	versprechen	to promise
zu	to	wissen	to know
		zeigen	to show

See also directions on pp.73–74.

OTHER USEFUL WORDS

◆ Foundation words

ziemlich	fairly
sehr	very
vielleicht	perhaps
wahrscheinlich	probably
meistens	mostly
mehr	more
nichts	nothing
niemand	nobody
jemand	someone
etwas	something
irgendwo	somewhere
irgendwann	sometime
irgendwie	somehow
sicher	certainly
sogar	even
fast	almost
etwa	about
auch	also
dort	there
beide	both
mehrere	several
zu viel	too much
zu viele	too many
wirklich	really
leider	unfortunately
die Leute (pl)	people

◆ Higher words

ab	as of
sonst	otherwise
außerdem	what's more
bestimmt	definite(ly)
dagegen	on the other hand
damals	at that time
damit	so that
ob	whether
einander	one another
falls	in case
gestattet	allowed
häufig	often

kaum	hardly, scarcely
schließlich	at last
seitdem	(ever) since
selbst	myself, yourself etc.
trotzdem	nevertheless
unbedingt	absolutely
verschieden	various
weder... noch	neither... nor
während	during
das Gegenteil (e)	opposite
der Gegenstand ("e)	object
das Jahrhundert (e)	century
die Menge (n)	crowd
die Möglichkeit (en)	possibility
der Vorteil (e)	advantage
der Nachteil (e)	disadvantage
der Unterschied (e)	difference
die Schuld	guilt
schuldig	guilty
die Regel (n)	rule
die Überraschung (en)	surprise
die Vorbereitung (en)	preparation
austauschen	to exchange
bedauern	to regret
bemerken	to notice
bestätigen	to confirm
bitten	to ask
dienen	to serve
erlauben	to allow
führen	to lead
gelingen	to succeed
gucken	to look
klopfen	to knock
schenken	to give
teilnehmen	to take part
träumen	to dream
sich verbessern	to improve
vermeiden	to avoid
vorschlagen	to suggest

97

Answers

◆ **How to learn**   **page 13**
Dictionary: 1 Brüder, 2 Tanten,
3 Katzen, 4 Augen

◆ **How to learn**   **page 19**
Vocabulary: 1 Ich räume manchmal auf
oder ich spüle ab. 2 Wir frühstücken in
der Küche. 3 Es gibt zwei Schränke über
meinem Bett.
Dictionary: Babysitter, Badetuch,
Badewanne, bequem, Bett, Blume,
Boden, brauchen, Bücherregal, Büffet,
Bungalow, bürsten

◆ **Kreuzworträtsel**   **page 22**
1 richtig, 2 Hausaufgaben, 3 vergessen,
4 Ahnung, 5 falsch, 6 Tasche

◆ **How to learn**   **page 29**
Vocabulary: 1 die Kantine, 2 die Stunden,
3 Englisch ist mein Lieblingsfach.
4 Es ist nicht schwer.
Dictionary: langweilig, Geschichte,
samstags

◆ **How to learn**   **page 36**
Vocabulary: Very useful: die Stelle, die
Firma, verdienen, das Taschengeld.
Less useful: die Schichtarbeit, der
Dolmetscher, die Bewerbung, die
Abteilung.
Dictionary: 1 Sekretärin, 2 Polizistin,
3 Kellnerin

◆ **Slogans**   **page 41**
1b, 2d, 3e, 4f, 5c, 6a

◆ **How to learn**   **page 43**
Vocabulary: der Anruf, wählen, besetzt,
der Hörer

◆ **How to learn**   **page 49**
Vocabulary: 1 head wound, 2 emergency
exit, 3 mortal danger

Dictionary: 1 fuel, gangrene, 2 to write
incorrectly, 3 pavement, 4 vote

◆ **Film titles**   **page 54**
1 *The Lion King*, 2 *Babe*, 3 *Live and Let
Die*, 4 *The Jungle Book*, 5 *Four Weddings
and a Funeral*, 6 *Sense and Sensibility*

◆ **How to learn**   **page 55**
Dictionary: 1 gewonnen, 2 geritten,
3 getroffen, 4 gesungen

◆ **How to learn**   **page 58**
Vocabulary: Gastgeber, begegnen,
vorstellen, ablehnen, Feiertag,
Gemeinde

◆ **How to learn**   **page 64**
Dictionary: 1 Streichholz, 2 Schlüssel,
3 besichtigen

◆ **How to learn**   **page 71**
Dictionary: 1 der Atlantik, 2 Kalifornien,
3 ein Pfund Sterling

◆ **How to learn**   **page 75**
Vocabulary: 1 feminine, 2 feminine,
3 feminine

◆ **How to learn**   **page 87**
Vocabulary: 1 crisps, 2 a skirt, 3 a biscuit,
4 a tin

◆ **Signs**   **page 87**
1 Im Sonderangebot, 2 Drücken,
3 Reiseandenken, 4 Obst und Gemüse,
5 Notausgang, 6 Einkaufswagen

Check your scores from page 84 …

Frage	1	2	3	4	5	6	7	8
a)	5	5	3	3	3	3	3	3
b)	1	3	1	1	5	1	5	7
c)	7	1	5	7	1	5	7	5
d)	3	7	7	5	7	7	1	1

0–12 Punkte
Du lebst nicht, du vegetierst. Trink erst einmal dein Bier aus und mach den Test noch mal. Wenn du dann immer noch so ein blödes Ergebnis hast, geh in eine Klinik.

Gib dir Mühe. Erst wenn du es schaffst, dir am Morgen mit ruhiger Hand ein Marmeladenbrötchen zuzubereiten, hast du das Schlimmste hinter dir.

13–25 Punkte
Nun ja. Du gibst dir Mühe. Du lebst wie du es gelernt hast und machst das nicht schlecht. Aber du bist gehemmt, du gehst nicht aus dir heraus. Du musst den Mut finden, den Kellner nach einer neuen Gabel zu fragen, wenn deine auf den Boden gefallen ist.

Tipp: Jeden zweiten Tag ein weichgekochtes Ei, weniger Kaffee, lieber mal ein Glas Sekt.

26–43 Punkte
Du bist in Ordnung. Wer so frühstückt wie du, lebt auch sonst ganz locker.

Du bist »easy going«: Was du zwischen 10 und 11 Uhr nicht schaffst, kannst du immer noch auf den nächsten Tag zwischen 16 und 17 Uhr verschieben.

44–56 Punkte
Angeber! Wir glauben dir nur die Hälfte deiner Antworten. Kultur und viel Geld sind nicht dasselbe!

Wer so wie du den Tag beginnt, mit dem ist etwas nicht in Ordnung. Wir verschreiben dir erst einmal schwarzen, ungezuckerten Kaffee, dann vier Wochen Müsli. Dann darfst du langsam wieder mit Schinken und Salami anfangen. Ist das klar?!

NOTES